RAIN BREAD

(A Book of His purpose and will from Heaven)

C 2022 TODD MARTIN BAILEY

*By The Holy Spirit leading directing me,
Todd M. Bailey witness of Jesus Christ*

If you purchased this book without a cover you should be aware that this book is stolen property. It was reported as 'unsold and destroyed" to the Publisher and neither the Author nor the Publisher has received any payment for this "stripped book.

Copyright ©2023 Todd Bailey

All rights reserved. No part of this book may be used or reproduced by any means, graphic, electronic, or mechanical, including photocopying, recording, taping or by any information storage retrieval system without the written permission of the publisher except in the case of brief quotations embodied in critical articles and reviews.

Because of the dynamic nature of the Internet, any web addresses or links contained in this book may have changed since publication and may no longer be valid. The views expressed in this work are solely those of the author and do not necessarily reflect the views of the publisher, and the publisher hereby disclaims any responsibility for them.

Paperback: ISBN 978-1-959533-90-0

LCCN: 2023912086

All materials used for this book was from the Author.

TABLE OF CONTENTS

Author Bio 5
Book Synopsis 6
Contributing Witnessing 8
Authors Forward Commentary 10
Author Dedication 13
To My Testimony And What I Started To Hear 20
BOOK ONE: THE AGE OF THE GARDEN 28
BOOK ONE: CHAPTER TWO: THE LORD JESUS CHRIST . . . 36
VOLUME TWO: THE RAIN BREAD POURED OUT 47
VOLUME TWO: CHAPTER TWO: OUTCOME 55
VOLUME TWO: CHAPTER THREE: SURRENDER 58
VOLUME TWO: CHAPTER FOUR: THE HOLY SPIRIT 63
V2: CHAPTER FIVE: THE HEART OF GOD 69
V2: CHAPTER SIX: LOVE 73
VOLUME 2: CHAPTER SEVEN: SPIRIT FILLED 81
VOLUME THREE: ONE WASH ONE SEAM: CHAPTER ONE   102
VOLUME THREE: CHAPTER TWO THE 'RAIN BREAD'
POURED OUT 110
VOLUME FOUR: CHAPTER ONE
THE GIFTS OF THE 'RAIN BREAD' 125
VOLUME FOUR: CHAPTER TWO: APECHO 130
Hear Me 149
Appendix 156
My Scope Of Prayer 157
Seven Shades Of His Light 158

Author Bio

Writer

Poet

Tunesmith

Songwriter

Artist

Day Dreamer

Goodwill Ambassador (Where God leads me)

Dad

Grandpa

Hobbies: Hiking, Fishing, Skiing, Camping, and Exercise.

Interest: Health, Education and General Reading

Love: Jesus, Family, Friends, and Pets, and the great outdoors!

Book synopsis

Holy Spirit led the Rain Bread offers its readers a sense of the Lord's coming. A place where heavens light shone through an ordinary man this book written on his heart came a river of light in the spirit. The author claim is only that from such an experience in Christ, he became a believer.

"…your young men will have visions and your old men will dream dreams…" Joel 2:28

"I am appreciative of believers who believe in Jesus without the doubt and reasoning I had as a non- believer. But I would have remained, sadly an atheist, without the intervention of our Lord and savior, Jesus Christ".

Although elsewise, my parents had me baptized and a few friends did a baptism in hope I would become a believer. I credit my wife and those who pray I might find Christ and by which my outcome began in Rocky's and Bobby's church, Times of Refreshing Ministry. Both word base pastors with rhema leading provided a chance for me to come to Jesus and eventually kneel before Him in the prayer of salvation. I accepted Jesus as my savior. And afterward I was baptized by the Holy Spirit and officially by Pastor Jack."

The point is all my life the presentation into Jesus life was made available. I had Grandparents who took me to their church. But as I formed I tossed out any notion Jesus was what was proclaimed and prophesized.

In addition to the action in such a read to effect no small stir… "To place my book in an era gone different is an act of endearment for Jesus who is the way, the truth and the life, as He declared. If nothing else…my love to draw onto to Him knowing He will draw on to me, as it was written. Jesus said, "Draw near unto me and I will draw near unto you; seek me diligently and ye shall find me; ask, and ye shall receive; knock, and it shall be opened unto you" (D&C 88:63).

"My following Jesus today is a walk in Christ; a simple walk. My faith placed me in fullness of His good news! I share it where I step."

CONTRIBUTING WITNESSING

This is a story, of a believer who is a strong witness, with a revelation that would be unbelievable....but it is truly believable, because I have been a part of it. My husband, Todd Bailey, is a living miracle of the grace and mercy of God. As an avowed non-believer, he was transformed into a "new creature in Christ Jesus". The Lord not only changed his heart, but dropped the Word of God into Todd's innermost being in a super-natural way! The "Rain Bread" is simply an insight and refreshment into the Lord's heart and will for these End Times. Glean what you may, meditate on the Word, and prepare for Jesus' second coming!

Pam Bailey

This little book is a call to action but probably not the kind you are accustomed to hearing today. Bookshelves are seemingly littered with all the self-help tools any person could possibly need to gain insights for getting ahead in this life. Nowhere is this more prevalent than in the religious section of any bookstore or online supplier! The one necessary thing, however, is what Jesus offered. Spirit and life, love and truth.

To those who had a deeper desire to hear a higher call, His words sparked a motivation to walk into the next life even while living in this one. Two sisters received Him into their home but one sat at His feet. Another woman encountered Him at a well where she eventually realized He was her drink. Outcasts became part of Jesus' in-crowd while big-timers were challenged to get small enough to fit through the narrow gate. Nobody is overlooked and we all have a story in God's epic saga.

In the end, all of us are like the rest of us, so listen for the Lord in this simple story of another and He will further His work in you. My wife, Bobbi, and I will never forget the circumstances of Todd Bailey's conversion to Christ. The hardened atheist husband who became the softest of sheep is one of my dearest brothers. His story will help you answer the call we all share – to follow Jesus intentionally.

Rocky Veach

rockyveach@gmail.com

Authors Forward Commentary

We all have to think through when we hear from God is it appropriate or vital to the works of Christ?

Also we need to give the space or notion of open mindedness while using discernment and in the open the room to be lifted up by God. God touches those He will for His purpose or will. I was lifted by His word and given more as if He filled up a new vessel with more wine. Anything is possible and He has done this throughout generations and literally made public his first divine miracle, new wine for the wedding He attended in His ministry here on earth,

Each answers that leading question to God and somewhere inside bearing on our inner most heart, we resolve purpose and meaning. We hope we come to His understanding and not our own. The world does it what the world will… but God's will, will open heaven on His time. Only the Father knows when Jesus will return.

When the time is right, I the Lord will make it happen.

Isaiah 60:22

My walk started a cross across my own yard in reverence, prayer and verse to our Lord. The Father, The Son and Holy Ghost led. In furtherance my walk went out to where I live in church yards, school yards, shopping centers, in my community praying for no crime and more God.

But as I pray the fruits of the spirit the light of heaven brighten at least what I could see against the duller darkness of complacency and tolerance for crime in our society.

Now a great walk God commands some of us, to walk in seeking higher ground for His church. For it is Jesus Christ who builds His church no matter how we attempt to develop church it is as Paul proclaims:

The Apostle Paul uses an agricultural metaphor for the church in 1 Corinthians 3, calling it "God's field"

What better way to express that but in the open?

So then, before God we walk as a church in the open field. I have heard to claim Jesus by claiming health to the land, the water ways, the habitats; human and animal and all living creatures in the open to The Father.

Be led in this walk by the Holy Spirit toward Jesus Return, Return Jesus. I heard keep your eyes on the heavens, your heart in God to perform this act of claiming Jesus at the cross and His resurrection upon His return.

The question is, "is there more wine to be poured?"

One has to answer that for his or her self. I believe so if it truly points to Jesus.

To place my book in an era gone toward indifference is an act of endearment for Jesus who is the way, the truth and the life. This is my love, my way to draw onto to Him, knowing He will draw on to me, as it was written. Jesus said, "Draw near unto me and I will draw near unto you; seek me diligently and ye shall find me; ask, and ye shall receive; knock, and it shall be opened unto you" (D&C 88:63).

I received barrels full of wine in the Rain Bread made by Jesus, if it were not so I could not witness false hope. For God gifted me and you hope eternal and everlasting. I have received barrels of wine in sermons from Rocky and talks with his wife Bobby and my wife, and with many other Christians, sisters and brothers. I have listened to many evangelist and many pastors to keep growing in the word.

Oh I heard at times through my life the story of Moses and Jesus… others preach, and or Hollywood makes a movie depicting the ancient times of Christ.

I saw "The Ten Commandments" staring Charles Hesston when I was a young boy. I went to church a few times with my folks and my grandparents but hardly kept awake, for lack of interest. I did recognize early on the importance people gave to their church and God. Yet, I formed a sense of humor about my early church experience that all of us were brought there to talk to the air. In a sense to clear the air…Sometimes rude laughter would overtake me. Who are they speaking to?

Author Dedication

Dedicated to: All men, women, babe and beast…..to these ideas; Zao, Zeo, and now Rheo… the flow, the fire, and balance of the Word of God, and to the Church Jesus is building, and the full body of Christ; to each member who knows Jesus, and to those who seek to know, and to each, their own personal relationship with God, through Christ Jesus. Amen.

My testimony and personal best going forward is to present what I was told as Heaven opened up for me: I am Todd Bailey. I testify that Jesus is my savior and redeemer. I testify God is alive. Jesus was resurrected and raised up the 3rd day for the remission of sin and forgiveness of sin so any one could be right standing before God, whom so ever believes in Jesus who as the son of God fulfilled the works of the Father. Having said this, I testify that I am a believer, now devoted to the Lord, as a messenger, witness and a friend.

Jesus took all sin upon him and cleared the way for each of us to choose Him over death and believe. We can choose to live believing and having faith in God to fulfill His promises. We have been given the keys to His kingdom to have everlasting life. God gave us a free will to choose and sin no more.

During my own quest to seek truth, and question God, in a pursuit of self-awareness, whereby one could think through God… Jesus showed up. This may slant or did bias my atheist view, there is no God, But this supernatural experience made what I did as forward thought, an exercise in compartmental thinking. I thought not unless by sight or hearing or by smell, or any combination of my physical senses, verified and checked against the reality of cause and effect did God ever exists. My logic was flawed to limits of the physical and my thoughts, I structured a perspective. Probing and questioning the possibilities of God existing or not existing I made a decision early in life He did not exist. In short my thinking didn't stand up to the Lord's presence.

Beginning in springtime of 1998, I began to have a number of "flash moments" by the Lord, along with encounters and experiences in the spiritual realm. I questioned the whole time what was really happening? And at times broke out in the laughter of my youth. You see I was a Dad and working in our family business.

My own Dad was self-made and entertained the great unknowable but he did not believe Jesus was any more than a man with a vision. Hard to believe today but at the time I adopted his point of view. But today I can say yes the visits happened. No one saw or witness these exchanges so it is my word or very possible His word in me so moved and I was a vessel or conduit. Either way some might say there are medical reasons for such claims, as I make today. Not sure what that means a brain mal-function or psychological need bent on who knows…maybe my heart crystalized from what the brain soaked up with those rare or infrequent church outings with family…can't say. I just thought at a very young age Jesus was a man that lived and he tried to lead people to a better way.

My grandparents also took me on rare occasion to their church where they sang hymns. I would go along in anticipation of escaping. I managed to grin and be in there company until we arrived back at the farm. Their farm was fun and my sense of heaven. I ate well as they were always putting out a table of goods and foods. I loved being outdoors and the smells of a farmland.

However, I arrived to Jesus; I was 45 and came to Jesus. Finally believing in Jesus, Jesus put into me this book. How do you do that?

I call it flash moments. There would be a bright light go off in my brain, always with the image of Jesus. Then nothing…then again something…word. Over time it would play out as a book. It has to be supernatural. I am open to other answers, it could be the brain somehow…we don't begin to understand the full capacities of the brain. The mind itself can imagine to a great extent and create all I have seen and heard. Or can it? Those things I never knew spoken before and yet I had new thoughts of understanding in Christ. Not my background of thought but thought produced by the new light in my brain and heart. Such as to look into the light and see heaven how could that be?

I do have a great imagination. But I will say I wasn't using it to seek Jesus. And no other guru, prophet or messiah did I spend my waking hours on. Get this, as far as that goes the only one who showed up and demonstrated Himself in all the religions and beliefs was Jesus. Jesus was there before me. It has its weight on the whole of what I went through to become a believer. It could have been any of the heads to any of the belief structures that claim divinity. Be it that, I am not divine, but seek as an ordinary person to be my own individual, and yet, my steps with Jesus became reality as I now follow. I always led by philosophy and liked the old philosophers for thoughts on conduct.

Prior to this, I saw myself in sports and possibly a career in sports. Then my interest in girls came later, my point I was a pleasure seeker. My hedonistic ways began to mature in college and set a tone as to how I went about living. In fact, much of what I wrote in the "Rain Bread", honestly I didn't have the background to know at the time what the Lord was having me write. Never questioned writing it either. I did know who saved me. That is the point! I was saved as thousands through generations have been, saved by Jesus Christ.

My ignorance of Jesus was astounding if to no one else but to me today. In my opinion, I had built up a disbelief of God that He took aim at. I am guessing as to how or why I would be visited by Him…Rocky the pastor asked me, "why you?"

I don't know the answer even today. Why not you? Or why not appear to just any person, for that matter. I am just that, a typical "any person". Average person at best but I will say on my behalf I love life! More so now in Christ, I see better greens and blues and can discern things better trusting God, if you know what I mean.

God can manifest Himself in many ways, unlimited really. And He has and He has appeared to others over the centuries. He has worked through others in every generation. Because, Why? He can…

Admittedly now, I had been living in darkness and unbelief for 45 years… knowing little of the Bible except as I said earlier, seeing Hollywood depiction's and occasional Easter Sundays with my family, we would go to a church. And then for me rejecting the testimony of Christ Jesus from those around me…up to the time I surrendered my pride. I gladly escaped these strange believers whenever I could. I thought they all needed a crutch or excuse to lean on to deal with life; a make believe God. A Santa Claus, a make belief construct to make us feel good and practice giving. And we all learn the truth about Santa. Unfairly I judged them. Definitely, I had a good case of ignorance.

Even so, I denied Jesus and making it difficult for my wife. I felt I was an unlikely candidate and certainly did not merit these supernatural visitations or flash moments of heavenly light, because I did not believe in the God of the Bible, let alone Jesus' resurrection. So even in the midst of recognizing something was up and I thought something was mysteriously wrong with me, my sense was I must be having a melt down and or someone with tech skills was playing a trick. I had the experience of going to Disney and seeing a holographic, I simply denied my first three visual experiences of Christ. Including those visuals formed inside Rocky's and Bobbi's church, at Times of Refreshing. The most important thing that I used to balance this out for me, was in all this time no other person or being came across for me and showed up so I could see, hear and smell. My room smelled fresh like outdoors in the woods. My reality was suddenly an illusion. Out of nowhere came a being from eons ago to disrupt me. I didn't know but using hindsight it could be the devil showed up using light to make an appearance like Jesus. It is strange, even weird, to think about it now against the backdrop of my experience with the Lord. I surly hid for a while because not from fear of others but fear I had an event I had no answer for. No background to check and no understanding to reason with.

What I later came to know, was that Jesus came to save me (and God had mercy and on me and my family!) as a result of the faith-filled prayers and confessions of my loved ones. But really in all candor He was there to give my wife lift where I failed her and myself and additionally. He was there for people like her; His people. Rocky called Him down and He appeared. I laughed and wondered how did this young pastor call Jesus down? Or more to the point what kind of high tech is this church into?

And no one saw the form of Jesus in any of my seeing or hearing. This made me validate old notions in me about church folks. This caused in me a bubbling of nervous laughter. Because, it was nervous laughter and not healthy laughter filled with confidence. My inner more sheepish person was not dealing with it. My veneer I put on was cracking. I found myself uncomfortable around church going people anyways and this made it worse.

I can't say enough about my wife's prayer work. Her strength, and reserve and character in Jesus amaze me still to this day. She was amazing to have put up with me. It was as if I was mocking her when I said I saw something behind the preacher that looked a lot like Jesus.

And ok, no one came forward and said they saw Jesus. Awkward! ...

Later on, about eight months later on, I had a real coming to Jesus. Sparing the details I can say the "'Rain Bread'" was imparted to me during this time (in an instant), but the work was instant and yet I have taken years to disclose, as I obeyed the Lord's call to write down that which He gave. He did not say put this book out there...I now know that it was not so much for me, but a good work, an inspired writing...a gift for His church, and those coming to the church.

Although, I often question (sometimes even doubted) the reality of the events of Jesus at the moment of belief...the presence of the Lord, the total transformation of my being, and continual confirmation found in the Word of God have overcome these doubts, in me. I cannot deny Jesus, I cannot deny what I have seen, heard, and experienced in the spirit. I cannot deny the gift of 'the 'Rain Bread'' and I find my time is now to share it.

This book is for each of His children, and those who need Him. But a big distinction is the Bible is the word of God and this writing is outside looking within. It is a work of heart and word that came into my heart. And one might ask, to what purpose? ... I could die with this writing not being printed and it wouldn't change the word of God or outcome of His will as it is written in the Bible or when He returns. The challenge ahead lies in receiving and working toward nothing less than the full representation of God's glory in His Church and the ages to come. I pray that you will receive this work as spiritual word, a light from heaven beaming forth through out the "Rain Bread" with joy, and constantly move towards this glorious outcome... for it is God's perfect will to build His church on Peter the rock and the words God put into Peters heart.

Jesus asked Peter, "But whom say ye that I am?"

And Peter said "Thou art the Christ, the son of God". Matthew 16:13-15

Jesus then said to Simon, "I also say to you that you are Peter, and I will build My church; and the gates of Hades will not overpower it." Matthew 16;16

The Rain Bread is to be tested and studied out to its spiritual message. The merit might be it was heard by me and He used my physical senses to reveal Himself.

He appeared on one occasion and said, "How can I serve you if you don't know who I am, if you don't believe, how is it I can believe in you, for only those who believe in Me will see Me in the days ahead."

That is where I began to learn about Jesus.

To My Testimony and what I started to hear

I testify: Jesus revealed the Father to me. The Father has put forth Jesus for all to see. Jesus is the first born from the dead. He died for my sins and all men. He lives so I can live and be right standing before the Father. He lives; that is the whole point to the resurrection in that without that event the story would be at best a "how to book, on how to live life; a guides book.

Through my wife and her faith in Jesus, Jesus worked and was manifested whole, complete, and within a heavenly light. But also it was through the two pastors and their church I attended that Jesus demonstrated who He is. Rocky was gifted and his sermons were alive with the Holy Spirit.

Jesus appeared and touched my heart, mind, and soul with these words of rhema and also His word as written in the Bible. In faith I walk with Him and by His high command, wrote these words which were promised for these times. Because Peter received such revelation that only the Father could of told him, Jesus claimed the building material going forward to His church. So you would know your God in ways that He is always with us. I know who I am and I am seeking the Lord my God in the name of His Son Jesus. Jesus is present always in the midst of our life as He said he would never leave us.

I was not given this message to cause fighting or division, but unity. Although, many churches in their individualize works, within their brand of retailing, their own brand of influence causes division. Even beyond the identification of Baptist, Lutheran, Catholic, Protestant or The Saints of Christ or numerous other denominations, and "born again" and evangelical churches.

I would advocate no influence in this work to be a thing separate from God. It is God. I declare it so because I know in writing it I listened to Him. My hope of its outreach be to cause curiosity in possibilities.

But God may completely define it differently and I am open to His leading.

Jesus builds the church. We all strive to follow Him to complete in us His work. We have Paul who exemplified and amplified the instructions to the church. Building the church is meant to be one church within the framework of God's gifts in the spirit to mankind. To catch this idea is vital, for in the end, it will be the church Jesus is building on Peter and the light in God of Peters declaration. The word down in Peter's spirit that came from God spoke the truth to Jesus.

To think otherwise causes division. Unfortunately, we fall under the influence of a spirit of division as sinners. The hallways echo our bias to what is practiced and what is truly said… Perplexingly, this has created many organizations and religious tapestries.

I was not anointed by Christ to argue the Word of God. Or in any way or fashion instruct the church. Or make claim the Rain Bread is the Fathers work and word. Yet, I have done so. It came from God.

Again, there will be many who say this is not their Jesus or their God. They will choose not to receive one word of it. I would only say to them doubt it for all it is worth and believe Him for understanding. Spirit tests the works and retests your own decision. Many will not receive one word of this work as set forth. The lord Jesus sent us the Holy Spirit, and the Lord gave His word to me for these days. I have not put this forth to convince you, but out of abeyance I have labored and performed the exercise to write as I was instructed.

God has spoken directly to me and this much I am certain, He so love the world He gave His only begotten Son as it has been written. These things were spoken to me by the Lord your God. I am only a messenger, a witness, and I am obeying Jesus Christ by His command. For He so named me in the presence of His Father His witness. For by His presence he came forth, and I have seen Him. He permitted me to see Him as He is whole of God. He asked me, "How can I serve you if you don't know who I am."

In that, I will see Him come and be among those who by faith gather before Him. God has opened a book from heaven so you could know it is your God. He told me when I went to Israel that He would not come by the wide Gate, but he would come by a narrow Gate, and only a few would pass through this gate with Him.

For this is what I heard the Lord say to me as I went forth to Israel:

Muhammad's feet are washed. Believe! I have washed every living soul's feet before they were. Every mother of every kind will clean a newborn. Not unless she is ill herself to her caring for her own. But every newborn that does not believe and those who deny me, die..

It is written more of Egypt would know me as the Lord, a sign for you to know I am. For it is a man without understanding that act on evil and believe he is made right in the sight of God. I was a sign for you to see that it is I. I will be raised and judged in My second coming the same as you. Even the greatest sinners amongst you and before you will be raised to be judged. The greatest sinners are those and or one of that in disbelief. I had said only God is good.

Yet you have not seen, and still you pray at your wall. How can the walls of stones ever answer you? They can because God can make them to do so. But then the wall would tumble as the wall of Jericho fell and God remained. Yet, it is also written My Father will reward your faith when you gather for My sake. I am that I am for My people. I am alive as I am Jesus. I will fill My wine sack with fresh wine.

I am here always and many who claim falsely to say they are me or I am out in the dry they are without presence of life, I am the life and I live.

It is not the work of My Father to bring a holy war into this realm. For only murderers would think to do that. A man of God can seek *the Father. To know the Father then you would know the holy war is fought in the spiritual realm. For it is not your war, but it is our Father's, and I will come for judgment and not by anyone else is justice rendered upon Satan. It is My act. You cannot judge another, yet you still do.*

It is not war that you should seek, but seek Me and the Holy Spirit of My Father will dwell on the earth as in the days of the beginning. Only those who gather in the days ahead in My name will be wedded and married and they will know Me as Jesus Christ.

The unjust slain are risen in My name. Is this so hard for you to believe? I said let the children come onto Me. The children who come to Me are both boy and girl, so it is both men and women who are ordained to My calling. God made them both and it is never been different in His eyes. But it is to be like a child to know the grace given. I have said give to Cesar what is Cesar's and give to God what is God's. For you who have a hard heart I verily say onto you give to Palestine what is Palestine's. And know it is I who command you to give to God what is God's. For My light is upon all. And I will reward faith, even at its root. But the roots cannot stay in darkness without water, for even the root will die. Come I will make you farmers and you will plant in preparing for the breath of God in the earth and in your soul.

I am not a respecter of any…even the just slain will be raised and judged. Be in righteousness when I come and not righteous before God. For the pride of a righteous man will even point and judge God. It will not go well for this person.

The blood of My children will be used in the days ahead. From the decay of this world there will be a plague put on those vile, those in disbelief will turn to Me and call Me their Lord. I will restore them. Even Egypt will come and know Me as Lord. I will take the plague off from those afflicted and who can turn and seek Me. For I am Jesus and as it is written I will make myself known to Egypt. It is written in the scriptures that your Lord would send a Savior to Egypt. I will make myself known when they cry out in prayer. This will be for you to see the light of the Father so you will know who I am. I will restore My people and God's nation. And I will make manifest right from wrong.

Each nation when I come will know me and bow to the truth. Many will be without water and I will give them water in belief I am.

I have fulfilled the scriptures and now it is God's will unfolding that you should know these things come from His glory. The Rain bread is My promise given to you for these days. For it is written My spirit pours out. I will send one to claim God's nation. He who will claim the land married, give My truth, and another to gather the nation's largest hospitality mission, give My love. Then My people will claim Me their Lord and I will appear to them. My remembrance is for all, any man, so is My love. For all are made in the image of God. It is your God who puts forth His Grace for His glory. He is glorified by you who believe in Him. I give you His light on the word, know it is the Rain Bread, and it is for your strength and courage to be amongst your God in the days ahead.

I will raise my children, and all say yes, and even those who died so will rise from the dead. God's mercy is greater than you know. I am alive and no one else can raise up the dead for life everlasting, for I am the Lord your God and there is no other. Still you will not believe. Still only a few will rapture. Then I will come for judgment and the remnant, but narrow is the gate to your Father's heaven. Then will the Father bring the remnant of his beloved into heaven. It is my heart for Israel that the remnant be all the tribes united. Only through Me will you get to the Father, for I am the one who is alive. One will be like Peter amongst you so I will name him Peter. One like each apostle and so I name them as I am. Even more will come with new names who hear Me. Only those tribes united in My name will stand alive unto the Father gathered in heaven as the Sons of God, but each man will stand for Me are the Sons of God. I am your friend.

You have made many days; now make this day a heart for God. For it is still the day of His favor. For a short while you can repent, atone, forgive, and live among one another in love. But you cannot put off the Day of Judgment. Know to rapture before Him is all come in healing and seek His heart. For out of the heart all the issues of life come, and I will be with you.

Do not fear evil and stand strong believing in the call to God. For Muhammad and many like him are like many branches on a tree pointing to their leaf leaning toward the sun, instead seek the heart of God. Many in seeking do not find it, for I am the heart. Do not fear men who seek God differently than you do. I will not know you the day I come if your heart is not seeking God through Me. All they need say is yea. I am the staff and I have given Myself to any man. For all can claim their right in Me, and receive all that was promised from out of the Father's heart.

It is not life or death, for both are given birth by God, it is that you seek God with all your heart, soul, and mind. It is as told that you should love your neighbor as yourself. So you will know that it is I, I command thee to love the heart of God unto all life. For it is written to love Him with all your heart. It is written to love your enemy. Make not a grave of His garden. Seal not His gate. Make a place for yourself on earth among the living for I will first come for life among the living, and then the dead among death who trusted me to come.

Scatter the bones away from My path. Many will come with faith in God, even Satan will walk as a mimic and put on he is Holy among the Holy of Holies, but none will hear a killer's plea, for all time murderers without repentance will be forgotten and left in the pit of hell. But I say even thieves, rapist, liars, adulterers, and those against the Holy Spirit will walk to see the Holy of Holies before only death. Judgement is not what you think or want but what The Fathers will is against His enemies.

Now make way and clear My path. For I have given of God's Rain Bread, so the hidden manna would be known. And you have no excuse. Bring it to life, as I have done, and be healed. I command each river to flow into one and come through the east gate and out the west gate and into the land where My blood now flows. I give My messenger this gift to write guided by the Spirit of My Father's gift to all life and any life. For My messenger will proclaim these things amongst you and you are to act in love. Begin to gather for the heart of God and let your hospitality be known to those kin to God.

Now give the wine and bread to those who will gather, and I will be among you. Let the breath of God come and flow the river through the center of the earth as you together flow by His glory in the earth. Then come the Kingdom of Heaven upon the Kingdom of God and raise up the land of the earth to His Garden. These words I set forth verify Me and confirm Me to affirm I am that I am. The messenger is not me and God will judge him like any other the day of judgement.

For those who hear, let the sun rise on this. You will come and go as you have done until the day you honor the command My Father has put forth. Love one another and love the Lord your God.

So you know that it is I am, when you are raised up in me as My body ever higher, and you cannot receive an act of kindness, then you have not been raised up in Me. For it is God's kindness, mercy, and forgiveness for all that any of you are given eternal life and the kingdom of God. I have told you love one another as I have loved you.

Book One: THE AGE OF THE GARDEN

THE AGE OF THE GARDEN

And this was what the Lord your God told me who believes in Him and all that has been revealed through the ages until now. I attest witness to such revelation in receiving the Holy Spirit. For it is the gift of His that we could receive in us the Spirit of God by the Holy Ghost.

The Lord said, "Speak to what becomes unto you in My name Jesus. You, who are good in your heart, so fill your heart with the goodness by seeking the Word of God, hear and see today by what is revealed in the Word; the new faith is the old faith, not hidden but born again and the old faith is the new faith, lived, it is life intended. For it is your God that effects your cause, and it is by the Father, your God, that although you effect your being to life and have a free will to choose, His spirit is My life, and I am the life.

Know this to be truth; the will of the Father is His love. I am your cause, and by what you effect here on earth, may it be the coming of the Garden, where heaven and earth meld into the firmament.

After signs…

After appearances…

After miracles…

After manifestations…

The sustained Christian reigns before the dawn of My coming… sustained by the will of the Father; perfecting the Garden, until I come. Until I come, don't worry nor fear Satan, but believe in your Father. My father perfects Me and I perfect in My body such things of His Spirit in you who take of My body and blood. God has always shown you His grace… He does the same today. It is still the day of such favor. My Father reigns in heaven and earth and by His will; ask and it shall be given unto you, so long as you stand in faith and obey His grace. Know where His grace precedes you, and walk toward it, pressing into God, and you will live aligned to His will.

I am Jesus, Lord as I am, and the throne is open to you, as you walk in God's kingdom. Still, you will never see the kingdom living in sin. Yet, you sin and stay merry for your short life. I told, "Blessed are the poor in spirit for they shall inherit the kingdom of God".

Life is given without sin, but life is dwarfed by sin. Use your will to discern which life is for you. I am the life. I am of the Father. This is God's gift that you have a will to discern and make of it your way to His perfect Garden. An open heart will see God, and it is in that heart that God will flow Me. I am the head of what I have become unto you, and it is justice. Give My body then, peace, and love, for I will come to make right those standing in the light of the Father. Be prepared and be of such faith, as justice favors only those in God.

You who can't discern, prejudice becomes you, pride befalls you, and you are left standing in indifference. Satan will confuse you in a world of indifference. So what is made easy before your God is to repent of your sin, and temper your nature with patience, tolerance, and longsuffering. These things have been asked of you who are still the stiff necks of your past blood. Get beyond this and open your heart to Godly ways, and attributes that become you. God is your friend, as He has given of His house of angels, and kingdom, and Spirit, and now Me, and now a Holy Spirit, for what is now His birth. I am the life.

Only by faith and an open heart can you see or hear Me; blessed are you who see God for you have an open heart. All will be open when I come, and I will come, but few of this generation will walk past the gates of heaven. Sin is so great today that you hurry the work of Satan. Greater it will be tomorrow, as it has been told. Give all you can to God, pray for His mercy, repent and stem the tide. For the last remnant will be risen in My coming, and I will come for justice, for those who stood for the Father or against the Father...

The last of you will be the first and the first of you will be the last, for it is My servitude of My Father that makes this so. I tell you the truth, what is given by My Father...is eternal life, and forever God is served by your having a relationship with Him. Ask who created you, both heaven and earth, and seek His answer. For He will always answer you if you seek Him...Everything is revealed to you who seek His answer. For He will always answer you if you seek Him...Everything is revealed to you who seek His truth. His truth like His glory is forever. This is how great a God, He really is. Not in all ways will you understand as a child made in the image of Him, the Lord your God, but from out of the dust you came and to there your body returns. Stay in His Spirit and be raised as a redeemed soul up to heaven. Gain your heavenly place among the living. Now heed no more to sin. But still you don't believe. You come to My church, and believe it will get better for you by being in the fellowship of My believers. I will separate pure of heart from those who are in cloak and hidden. I see all hidden things upon the heart, so beware.

Run through passages throughout the ages by God's will. From the beginning to the end, and during all kings, and all prophets, and all holy men and women boomed the Word of God in all works done and all works to come. Shout and proclaim it! God's Garden! And it will be revealed.

The fruit is perfect and given unto you in My name's sake; take of it and be perfection. The forms to appear will heal the world of its woes. Those forms are from My Father's heavenly realm. His sounding rings truth!

The bugles over vast expanse in array of patterns, color, tones, and voices of heavenly creatures, creatures of your Father's, will amplify the anointing of life given you to sustain you. As I have foretold, draw closer to God and He will draw closer to you. The issues of life will flow apparent from out of the heart. I am the heart.

The fullness is here…now seek it. Harvest the fruits of the Garden that your Heavenly Father has set before you, that you have not touched or seen or witnessed. Behold, before you is the tiller and the time to seed the Garden is now. Make your every step forward toward the Garden and bring those things that will bring alive the health of the world. Rise up complete health in all things. Read the Word of God; live as I have told you. Face My cross and believe I have died, so you may live. But I live now so you may have life. It is all written so you would understand. Come now and walk barefoot in My kingdom. The kingdom of My Father is at hand. It is truth, complete beauty, and whole, and just. Your church will only be as strong as your weakest member and your weakest member could appear to be your stronger member, if you yourself fall where they do not. In My kingdom all are strengthened by faith. By such faith, the kingdom comes. I am He before you. My kingdom comes and prevails, and all goodness works through My bread, and the rain I pour out gives My bread rise to its dough. For My rain flows fire and balance like a good oven. I will perfect the heat that no side will fall.

My church will seed the largest gathering of My people, and they will bring forth the largest hospitality mission and grow up the Garden's first complete ring. So then, what is a ring will be engulfed and grow quickly into God's Garden. For it is from the Garden that God comes forth.

And of its flower given over to a bloom, My will be done as your Heavenly Father commands. I will walk in the Garden with you, and take you over to the apple, and you may eat of the apple, but you will not die, you will not falter, you will not suffer, for My suffering gave you deliverance and life. God has given you the right to taste the apple and be forever knowledgeable in His heavenly kingdom. For it is written the earth is His; God's field!

All of this is just so, because God loves you, and all who seek the Word. As you may love and flourish in the era of springtime, so will come the rain and the sun making the climate for sustaining you in God's heaven and earth. I will be the sun and the rain, and I will do great things in God's name when all the gardeners can be accounted for, and your earth is made ready by seeding the outcome of a great harvest.

The Garden's brilliance gains beauty as truth stands whole of Israel, whole of the land, the Church, the offering, the covenant, and the body. I am, all those things made whole…even in you, and so you could be made whole of the Father. I will appear in wholeness, a glory cloud to God, and at that time, heaven will be shown to you. I praise God that upon My return all of the world will sing His praise with Me and all that can hear will be saved. All nations will be Israel. I am the center of all Israel. And Israel is the land where God will roam and be heard. And praise God that He may hear your praise in His garden. The Garden birds and His essence will be made in song and be made comforted by your love and praise and spirit. The land will uphold all those saved by belief, and by the acts of honor abiding by the laws of the Spirit.

Wait My second coming and I will not come in your time? If you wait until the sun comes up an goes down, and the planting season goes by, then you will starve, for your crops will never come in time for the harvest, especially if you never plant them. Ask not what My coming will be like, or when I come, or by what means; none of this is important. For is it this year or next year, or what is the time of the prophecy? For time is God's and He make of it what He will. For only the love your Heavenly Father and for your neighbor matter, and are important to Us. These are the commandments set forth in life by all His prophets, and as I am. I am the life. I am in the Father and the Father is in me. So believe in me and I will be in you also. I sent down the spirit of truth to guide you. Be guided by the Holy Spirit. Take up your mantle in God.

But if you plant today those seeds given, and those seeds by His Word given life, and those seeds given by His fruit, and live by the laws by which you are put forth, then what you can harvest tomorrow will be your victory. I tell to all those who will listen, that I will walk in the Garden with all those who now plant and seed His Word; you will see Eden, and be with God who loves you, and with Me who also loves you, and His Spirit who also loves you. Don't fear calling to Us for we hear your prayers. But only God's will, has ever answered a prayer. I lift your prayers to Him. So when you pray believing, believe in the will of God by the power of His Word. What is stored up in heaven will come pouring out, and the flood of His righteousness will be upon earth, as it is in heaven, at the instant I come out of the glory cloud. Stand in God always. It is the day of His outpouring.

Call the Garden down. Reach out to God's Eden, and make of this world an image of Eden, and then I will be amongst you. I am Jesus, the Son of God, the firstborn, your intercessor, and the moment between you and the Father. For I am the moment coming of God, and you who are pure of heart will see Me.

Seek your outcome by seeking the moment of God and it will be My coming as natural as the heavens open and the rain pours. I am caring for God's Garden and waiting for the tillers, farmers, and the caretakers. You are made in the image of God, thrown out of the Garden by Him, but given redemptive rights in My name. You only need to seek, and you will hear Me, and see Me till the soil for you. The fig tree has stood near two thousand years among weeds. There will be weeds always, until the last day. But if you truly hear, pull your own weeds. Attend to your people and weed your own garden, until your garden grows within His Garden. Work to make the earth healthy in God's. Believe in the Word the health of the Garden. Allow your Heavenly Father to show you. God will bear fruit of such substance never before witnessed, to sustain those who flow and groom the Garden for the wedding. When I come, all will be lifted to heaven who tend the Garden in My name. I am Jesus and I am alive.

Plant yourself in the Garden and make good the soil by seeking God. Be good servants. I serve this servant whom I touched to be truth. He writes all I have asked, and does all I have asked, and for that he will be in My kingdom, and his heirs, family and those yet to be counted, who know that he has written My truth. Yet, he still will be judged for no man misses God the day He comes for judgement. All is forgiven who believe in Me and do the will of the Father. Fear not judgement not unless you continue to walk in sin with a false heart for God.

Your God has blessed you and your place in His Heavenly Garden. So in return, do the same for the Father in your own backyard, and make the world in Him. I am His image so be like Me and it will go well for you, for you will see greater things in His image than Me.

He so gives, to My body His hospitality. And in return, from His wine, I press in, and from the fruit of His Garden, you receive His blessings. So, this day know the abundance of His blessings… Blessed is he who sops up the wine with His bread and gives of it to the Newborn.

Blessed is he who labors the works in the Garden and farms the land, and brings forth the grain to those in need.

Blessed is the fig tree, which bears up God's fruit. It bears fruit for all those who make it into the Garden. How great the fig tree will be if all who believe will enter, believing in Him who has made the Garden for you; for you will always be fed and served in My name, His hospitality.

Blessed is he, those of you, who churn the soil and fertilize it with My Father's blessings, for My deed is the abundance of your harvest. You will feed My nation.

Blessed is the one who sustains the Garden in My name. For those of you, who so work in God's will, will be sustained forever.

God hears your prayers for those prayed. God has written in the book of life those you've prayed for who do not believe, but do-good works. For they will make at least; paradise… God will judge them still, but I will take up with Me their burden of non-belief before God. For My cross still stands. By the cross, even they are given a chance to make it in heaven; still, as near to an end, they must choose Me, for I am the Shepherd who leads the sheep to God…or as sheep go astray, be lost and fall prey to the wolf. Say yes or no, but nothing more than need be told.

I have told it before: you must believe in Me; believe in the blood covenant, My blood shed for all of man, My blood before God to attest that you are worthy, and that you have been freed from sin. This is the agreement your Father requires of you.

I took all your sin to the cross that day, so why would you attract more sin, when you can be free to live a sinless life. Isn't it better to be lifted up than dragged down by evil? You are redeemed in God for My sake, and you will enter the gates of heaven and rest with Us beside the quiet water. In heaven and on earth, and always in life, you will truly live with no scourge.

I tell you the truth; God is a just God. But those who walk away, and live in between belief and unbelief, it will be hard for you to see God that day. Even as I come, those of you who will not believe, I will not know you. I do not return to be known to all, but I come to bring everlasting peace, and triumph over darkness. I will not hesitate to push the darkness away, and burst forth with the Garden of God. All His glory will reign and I will be back with My beloved children. I am your friend.

Book One: Chapter Two:
THE LORD JESUS CHRIST

"What is of this world that is Satan's is dead, but what is dead to God is the death of Satan. My coming is not the death of Satan, but the breath of life in God. Satan's death is Satan's; who suffocates, who's fire consumes it. But your death is the redemptive life in God, if you so choose. In My coming, heaven will fall upon the earth, and all who believe in God will be washed in My Rain.

All believers will be given their rightful place in God's Garden. But beware; times will not be without tribulation, and the punishment of dead souls. In My coming, it is God's will. It is God's will that you will receive My coming. You are the living body of Christ and you have been promised the fullness of God's abundance, and God's fruit from within the Garden of Eden. You have received as it has been told, joint heir with Me, and your needs supplied, and all the riches in the glory of God.

Yahweh comes and fulfills, for perfect hearing are the sounds to His name. Prepare the way for My coming, for I will come and the earth will be restored in My name for God's sake, that He may also come and walk with you in His Garden.

Satan has confused the world of what is man or what is Satan, but what is God's can never be confused; for it is love, and health, and life living prosperously in the Word. Don't be confused, don't let the world mount up against you. For it is I, who in the will of God come forth to make all evil perish.

God reveals an essence in all things. But beware that Satan can manifest in this world a likeness to God, thus drawing you near to his den and trapping you inside his rage and his confinement of hatred, jealousy, lust and death. So great is Satan's hatred that even the dead fear his death with extreme frenzy. But God draws near to you by love, as you draw near to God, rejoice in His name with true fear, with reverence worthy only of God. For this you are blessed and will have been received and given the rewards of God's love. When you pleased God, He is well pleased and given freely unto you is your inheritance in Him. God is pleased when you sing praise and receive Him.

Praise God; for God's pleasure is to give to you for loving Him. God's measure of pleasure is your receivership and guardianship of the Lord your God's love. Your Heavenly Father's will is done in you in My name when you give yourself to Him who cares for you. Look to God's will and call to it, for God hears you when you give yourself to Him who cares for you. Look to God's will and call to it, for God hears you when you pray believing. I am Jesus who bears your cross and lifts in you, your resurrection to god, in God, by His Word. I say to you, you can gather God's wheat, and make bread, and feed yourself; gather

His fruit and drink God's wine and have all that God sustains in you by fellowship, and by My hospitality share the good news as you walk in God's love; all this is added unto you through Me in Him, your Heavenly Father. But you cannot have all this, and the breath of God, nor the air of His essence, nor God's plan, nor God's will, nor a relationship with God, if by your action you worship anything revealed to you that is not His Word. Only in God's Word, can you inherit through Me, the kingdom of God. For the heart of God is in the fruit of His Word. Travel as you must by the Word of God; for this is the only way you can travel to heaven. His anointing is in His Word, and all power manifests itself by His Holy Creation.

In all great feats of man by God revealed, make certain that the product of your mind does not contaminate, pollute, and make toxic a wasteland fitting only of a place Satan can walk. The will of God is born out of His heart, and to know this is to perfect your hearing. I am the life. I am the life without sin.

It is God's will that the earth be of heaven, not of hell. The light of My Father traces out from all circumstance, and from such events, His will be done. All the health of God is bestowed upon you. The earth is yours to cultivate a path for God to walk. What has been revealed as spiritual destruction in the Book of Revelation, will be healed and made whole by God Almighty, and in My name it will be the glory of My father upon the land before evil's wake. God will come bearing the gifts of life, as He has forever and ever. He so loves the world and you who dwell in His name, and then God will annihilate evil to its end for all time, giving you His peace. It will be done.

I will come on His horse, but it is not a horse that you know. I will judge evil to its end and by Him raise up by His love, His people, and all of Israel. Although you do good work nation by nation, and church by church, there will only be one nation and one church restored, and that will be the land of Israel. Israel will conquer all nations and all churches. For it was never to be a nation against God. It is His nation; still a mustard seed in belief, and His nation will rise up above all others. Let it be said, "God's will be done".

All of Israel is God's Garden. But you know not yet, what Israel is, all of Israel is God's heaven, however, you know not yet, this to be His truth. All of Israel is God's domain over all things. All of Israel is all there is to the universe, and all dimensions therein beyond all there is. Israel is the land by which God created both heaven and earth. Israel is the Nation of the universe and the glory of God. I am Israel, the center of your realm. The heart of Israel is God. But you take the name in vain. You name a small country Israel, but it was all Israel spoken to His glory. All Israel fell out of His Spirit, and all of His Word went forth to create heaven and earth. Still you don't understand this, and you won't until the day you are in heaven.

Let this be said, "Oh Israel, will you not rise up to His glory in Me?"

I will tell you a few parables, so that you will draw closer to God and not to meaning or understanding, but to God's essence, and by the breath of God, you, by His grace and glory, receive the first signs of My coming. Breathe in God as you look to see the open door to heaven. For it is by the breath of God, that life was created. And so it is today, when you breathe in the Spirit, by breath, you are receiving life.

A man who lives amongst you drowned his own family. He repented of his sin by asking Me for forgiveness. I told him, they did not drown, and because they believed, they flowed from out of the river of God. But you, who murdered cannot come to the water and be baptized in My name, unless you in repentance come before God asking forgiveness and believe in Me. You who can murder and ask not for forgiveness have drowned in your own mud.

Still, you judge and do not think to forgive. So it is your system and not your Father's. His Holy water brings forth the root of the fruit that sustains life. Only once will He judge you. Yet, He has forgiven you forever. Very few of you heed to this to know it to be truth. Those of you, who forgive very little, will receive far less. I tell you, most of you know the way of the world, but forgiving is beyond many who know of its complete work. Forgive in My name and receive complete the Grace of My Father. Yet, many of you will laugh at this, and not know that I gave you the power. For the power of God is life. I am the life.

The Word has already been written, so only I can add unto the Word, but My Spirit is the truth in the Word, and I am alive in Israel. The truth is already written. Nothing is yet added only more light is given.

Still, few of you understand this to be so.

There is only one God to be hallowed by all, as to perfect your ear to hear, so that you have a perfect will. The path that triumphs is His. Still you don't understand. The life in His Word is alive, and by His Spirit, quickens you who seek Him. I am He when I am Israel, the light of heaven and earth. I know His Will, and He wishes you to take of His fruit and fill with His grace. Bring no harm onto another. For how great is your sin, if you worship anything before His grace. If you act against your God, then who are you in the end without Him? For nothing is nothing.

Your days are numbered and by God's essence many signs will now unfold as foretold by the Word. If you bear fruit to God's Word, El Shaddai will sustain in you the Holy of Holies, and you will bear witness to things not yet made visible, but yet by El Shaddai's voice, you will hear only what was heard at the beginning of time and see to what end God comes to live amongst you, who through Me prepares the way. Look not for miracles or signs, although they become apparent and abundant as heaven nears to this world. But seek God and all God's plan that binds heaven and earth to you and to Me, by the Holy Spirit, and to our Heavenly Father. Believe, it is easier for you to die than to live. Yet, to live is everything and to live by His eternal love, is a gift unto you, and given to Me.

To some of you who engineer and design and, say, "it is God-revealed", you abuse the substance, and your God waits patiently for you to come and receive the full answer. I tell you the truth: you have the answer, and His fullness. For it has been revealed since the beginning, yet you, who walk away with the substance like a child who loves sugar, who, if not guided will take too much sugar an become sick, so it is with you, who designs a jet that burns up the ozone. What do you do? You put more jets into the sky until the ozone is depleted. I say to those indulged, "Like the child who takes too much sugar, and will suffer, so they will suffer the groans of this earth. This is true of you who burn the forest to the ground, building temporary housing, you cause other parts of the world to be scorched and yield a desert. So it is, ever since the time you walked away from His Garden. I tell you so you will raise up to care for each other and for God's earth. None of you are good stewards of the planet, of those who rake the planet and don't heal and reclaim it to God. Even though you claim you are in God, believing in me. God gave you a will to take care of His earth. I tell you the truth: all His love that is added unto you by the Father is life. I am the life. So why would you ever take away from life?

You believe you must take to get, and the thing you get is the taking. Give and you shall receive, but still you try to take more, until you get nothing. You who are the taker's still don't know what you do, and by such design is destruction foretold. Take only what you need to live with God and be filled with His joy of you. Then in your abundance, give and it shall be returned unto you 10-fold, and some even 100-fold. For My glory is the glory of God in you, and that you want for nothing, and your needs are filled.

And those of you who receive from God, the Word, but ignore His word, even in partiality...you will not see the beginning of God upon the earth at My second coming. It will be hard for you, even though you've revealed God in many ways, such as "$E=Mc2$", to ever be included into the Garden of Eden and in heaven. All the destruction will be given unto evil and unto you for your part. To be in half belief is no belief. God's earth is the direct path to God's domain, so make of Her your health. Grow the Garden; don't spoil its fruit by eroding the soils given to fertilize the seed. Where you use the earth put back into the earth until the day God restores the earth.

Now, let Me talk to those born with afflictions. Those born out of suffering, those who die stillborn, and those who live as if all of hell is upon them...I say to you, "God absorbs you". As I absorbed all sin, so He perfected My Spirit, and absorbed Me in His love, and by His grace all sin was purged. It is truth: you choose life or death. So know this, it is true for you since the day of My resurrection. By your faith you are perfected in life to live, and by such power you are absorbed in Me ...your passage to the Father's heaven.

You, who have caused none of your misery, like the oceans that receive toxic waste, God will cleanse you in God's time, by grace, and by the supernatural touch of His hand, and heal what is in the land, and people. He will eliminate all poison and toxic waste, if you will it to be so, and act by His will to do so. In that day will come a cleansing of His people. Know this, you are absorbed complete cleansing of your spirit, and by the Father, you are perfected in Me as life everlasting.

You are like the man or woman who has stumbled upon fertile land, but they haven't one seed among them to plant; so destitute are they to starve and suffer while walking upon the fertile ground, that you would say they are hopeless. But they are not… if God can breath life into a man, so will He absorb life in all its unjust sufferings, because God is just. All unjust suffering will be restored upon My coming.

You will become a new creature and shed your misery unto evil. God will penetrate you by God's glory, and I will walk with you through heaven's gate. We will be together in God's Land. I will take you by the hand and we will walk together with God. Know this, it is given: you have received God's gift and are spared by His forgiveness in you. God knows of your affliction. Although you may not hear or see Me, God has graced you by His love, and you are healed in My name before Him. Believe Me when I tell you that there are ways to absorb an unjust, like an oil spill or a broken promise. I absorbed all sin against you, yet the sin of the world chokes the very tree of life by the will of others who will not obey My commands. But a time is coming and God's will be done…justice will serve those in Me.

God gives many chances by revealing, by His Word, His light upon your life. It is time to understand His light upon the Word and its power upon you.

So understand, let this be known: God can absorb all the radiation. Yet, God will not absorb in whomsoever, one molecule of radiation released by whomsoever for destruction. Woe to anyone who uses radiation for destruction; God will return all and more radiation upon you and stand you in the fiery pit of hell for eternity. What you know of radiation, is nothing compared to the burning of hell.

Whosoever unleashes radiation to destroy the world, or one thing of this world, will receive such heat that evil's own flame will engulf them beyond belief. You know how good belief is, if you receive everlasting life…I consecrate the ground that all life lives. Find your way to honor life by giving a way for such life to live. Clearly, now you have been told. So there are no excuses. A life that lives to give life the joy, endurance, love, and peace to live; is now given My power to receive the will of God. The Word will overcome you and you will be in heaven by His glory and light. Be filled now in His light and receive My power.

Now, whosoever cultivates the Word of God upon the earth, like a farmer who hears, will produce from earth's soil, such rewards. Forever the wonders of God will flow forth and His garden will be without thorns and thistles. But he who lays barren the earth, robs her of her resources, leaves her oceans distilled of life, and pollutes her land by making it a toxic wasteland, I fear he will not like God's promise; he who destroys the earth, harkens the call to Satan, he will walk one mile with Satan forever in the pit of hell's fire. Yet I say walk two miles with one who ask you to walk a mile here on earth.

Hear Me well then children of God. I have spoken these Words. I so name a new teacher, a servant of the Lord, those believing are each My servant as I am a servant to them.

I have written these words so that you may not be surprised when I come. Whomsoever I have inspired is no more special than you who believe. But whom I have named by friendship, are we not all friends? So, we are each a friend of the Father, for what child does not look upon his creator with admiration…

I proclaim, with two, one comes to call the Garden down to earth. By him, God is served "Christian hospitality" and to those who hear him, will be Christians sustained by God's sustenance. One I name life, will cultivate and teach you God's Word. I will lead you into "Christian hospitality". Still all Islam and Jew will come by their own hospitality and it will be named a separate river "Islam hospitality" and "Hebrew hospitality". Still even so, all nations will have each a separate river named after them. But the river of the Lord your God's hospitality will be even greater and it will be called, "I am that I am". My river will heal, mend in love, and give force to cut all sin away. Bring even those captive, those sick, and those homeless and poor. The breath of God will heal them. The river I speak of is the river of God's power, yet you will never know this river by being separate. God alone can heal and restore the earth.

Now, behold one by which My coming will be shown through, and he will foretell of the fruit. Through him I will be called down and I will come down in the rain..."times of refreshing", and receive those first of My church. And one will call out the "Rain bread" by fire. And one will balance My Word and My Light, and all the hidden manna will unfold in these times. And born of this purpose he will say, "Behold the white light of the Father and the holy Men therein, therein comes the Lord, He is with Him."

For I will be in person that day and it is in I, that you will hear such sound of the Father. You cannot know of such things, so it is not easily believed. The mind cannot produce the sound, only by My Father's heart, can I come. It is the Father's heart that sounds out My name and My time to come. It is by heart, that you will see Me at all. The time is at hand when the Father opens the rains, and I say this is the day in your hearing.

I will not name My brother, so he who calls may not be persecuted, but by his lips alone the seal will be broken and I will come. I will come quickly, so those for my name sake are not persecuted anymore. You will say "come" and come you will to the Lord your God, and I will come to you and fulfill you with your Heavenly Father's will.

Volume Two:
THE RAIN BREAD POURED OUT

Glory be to God! This is what the Lord has told Me in the fullness of His glory, so that I may hear well and write well that which He speaks to … I pray you hear, as I have, and save your soul, by believing in Jesus, who came to redeem us, and who died for our sins. Pray to His resurrected self, for the life. Jesus is Alive!

The Lord speaks: "Those things that are to be…are of worldly life and may perish as the days go by, but those things of My will are of heaven, and what is of heaven is God, and God lives forever. Those things of this world are given to man, and it is only by the authority vested in man, that this world can be made better. Only God gives that authority in life to live. But it is only by God, that you can draw the world closer to life, He longs for you to have life and a relationship with Him as a friend. This is the way in heaven and earth. And it is only heaven that can heal the world, but you can maintain it and sustain the earth. Through Me and by Me are you received, by My authority in heaven and on earth; but if you are of this world, and not of God, nothing will be your name, and nothing comes of this world for you. You see the world one day and you will not see it the next. So when you seek God, seek Me, and I will receive your work, and your prayer, and I will tell it to the Father. I will know you by My name, when you walk in My love. For My love is God's love. I will know you for your good work in My name. I will know your knock when you seek first your Heavenly Father, and by the Holy Spirit, so then I will take your call to the heavens and intercede on your behalf. Pray you must to God; if you wait on life and prolong sin, not even a whisper is your name.

God told you I was His Son, and that He was well-pleased. Now hear, as I hear, "My Son is My heart of glory, and all glory are My children, and My brother's and My sister's witness to Me and I witness unto each, I am pleased. For this I give My gift that all can wash and be fed the light upon My Word". I hold all things together of this universe. Now, I speak of those things that are to be prior to My coming, so you might hear of those things your Heavenly Father wants you to have on earth. On earth, as it is in heaven…I spoke it and it is so. The Spirit of God has never left the earth or your hearts, those of you who pray believing. I am the way to the Lord your God. I have taken your sins upon me at my crucifixion and cast them back into the bowels of Hell. And the forgiveness of sins was shed by my blood. Yet many still sin.

God reigns, sounding awe, and beauty, and all you have to do is look inside yourself, and center your heart in God's love. The fullness of His love is His kingdom, and this I am certain, it is the truth; you can have the kingdom today if you believe in His Word by hearing His sounding in fullness. God sounds the trumpet by everything that is His, but still you do not hear. If God is everything good, why wouldn't you want everything that is God's? Why do you defy God? For lust or greed or sickness, you keep company with the one who battles God and is dead to God. And what are those things? God has told you that, in sin, there is nothing but death. Mainly, you defy yourself and your sickness is overcome by nothing. To be nothing is your fame. There is no glory in becoming nothing. There is no comforting sound in nothing. There is no fullness of God's measure in you and therefore you are not even the dust. You, who will not believe will never have lived. When you look into the space of heaven, you do not exist. When you look into the space of the entire universe before you, you do not exist, if you don't seek God first. This is damnation!

God's measure has always been to bring men and women and children into God's Garden, but not without salvation and trust, in faith. Now, you have redemptive rights inherited in your name with God, and all that is requested from you is your faith in Him who gave His only Son for you. Beware, it is either a man with no vision of God, or a woman with no hope of God, or Satan, hard at work to keep you from what is God's, and what God wants you to have. Yet still, you defy God, after all that has been shown and all that has been done in My name Jesus. For My name is His name. It is the only name by which you can stand before Him. I give My blessing over what is good in My name. A good man or woman who believes in God is in the fullness of God's glory. His goodness will overcome! But the fullness of His glory is given only, when your heart is opened and purged of all sin, left pure-hearted in God Almighty. Give Satan back his sin and fill your heart with God's glory. Don't make your foundation one of sand, for what is sand will be carried away in the wind.

The sound of His Word frees every blockage in the heart; so hear, and break from death. Know well the words of God. Your Heavenly Father uses His breath of love to breathe into you life, and of this life you live only to be a beautiful truth, made in His image. God has asked only for your love surrendered in faith, and all received will all be given, all His eternal glory... but still, you go your own way. Your heart is hard.

Now you should know this: I speak to those not believing, for the believer has received the sounding of the Word, and the believer only needs to follow the Word of God and stay in the Word of God forever and ever, that he may flower in fullness of God's glory. Fullness of God's power comes to anyone in My name who has a pure heart and a quest to seek God in His glory. Few of you believe in such glory, and when you enter paradise; you are deceived by your own heart. You believe that paradise is the

Garden. The Garden of God is in Heaven, and Heaven is in His glory, and His glory is in you, who can hear the Word sounding in the fullness of God's love; know paradise is not the Garden, but just a little ways above hell.

There is no law, only fulfillment of the law, by those believing in Me. I came to fulfill the law. I have fulfilled the law and now you are free to hear; so those who can hear let them hear in My name and turn as they will to you and take your hand, leading you to My Garden. I extend My hand to you, and blessed are you who take it. Know this, as you know the blue sky or the sun above, the day will come and We will be of that day's glory, and not of legends, age old heroes, or stories of conquest, idolatry, or imaginations. We will be with God, and it will be God's will on earth, and all death will perish by His sounding glory. All sin will be gone.

Some of you still seek to move as God would move. Yet, you lock yourself away in ritual or rites, or you wear a cast instead of fine clothes that the Word weaves. Seek the truth and hear the voice of God. God sounds His Word in your heart and if you can hear move with God! Balance your life with life, and sustain the Word in your life. Then your life will reside in the safe harbor of your Heavenly Father. Move with God's Spirit over the water, through the air, and on land, and in life. The time of rejoicing is now. Speak My name and be joined within to the Spirit of God. For God will bear fruit and His gifts upon you. Those, whosoever give in My name, Jesus Christ, will receive in My name, ten-fold, a hundred-fold, and more. For I will multiply the fruit of the Lord your God! Call out your reverent fear of the Lord and be heard. Call out in My name and I will come. Justice will be served in the fullness of your Heavenly Father. I tell you the truth: God's heaven is bluer and greener than this world. If you can make of the earth a truer color of both blue and green, then you will see what awaits you in the Garden of God. You must work to produce a clean and healthy environment. Your earth must move toward God's glory. What is of this world is the world, but what is of the earth is God's earth. God owns the earth. Make of the earth a Garden, not a desert. Nothing, can grow in a desert that is not a blessing from God. Clear the path to God and God will descend upon you with His holiness. Your pursuit to make the world a better place is not in vain to God's will. The world will always be worldly until the day of My second coming. But have faith that you can bring the earth into God's will, and what is of this world will separate unto nothing, leaving you and the earth with your Heavenly Father, the Son, and the Holy Spirit. What is not the will of God is ambition other than God, and ambition not of God is of the world. Be careful that your ambition doesn't cut you off from the life that becomes you. Woe to you who severe the tie that binds you to God's love. You will succumb to your ambition, and that part of falseness you've exploited for yourself, will consume you. Beware! And the world of man who does not believe in Me, will perish forever.

When I come, you will have called, and God will have been answered in full. Although the Spirit of God will move upon you, you must be ready for all time to part ways with this world. God will separate you from the reckless, the twisted, and ill-fated fool given over to Satan. All that is of God, on My day, will be accounted for. Those saved will be delivered to eternal life with God, those in defiance will be swept further away and bonded to Satan. They will go the way of the pit of fire. Death will be overcome. And heaven will descend. From out of the spirit, the earth will be renewed. God will hover over the earth in those days and expand its lands and waters.

Now let Me speak to the arrogance of men who know of God, but do not seek God. You are in defiance. You know of God, but you are like one who smiles in victory but despises another for winning. You pretend to know God. You are like a snail traveling on the bottom of the sea; a poor fish will get to God before you do. I tell you the truth: that no man, woman, child, nor beast in God's eye is more important than another. Kill the beast you must to eat; be careful of killing for more. But someday, when all is restored you will not have to kill the beast or dig the soil. Glory comes to you in My name if you conquer Satan for righteousness sake. Beware, that it is not a false beast you've slain and then seek an honor for yourself. Satan will draw you closer to his table and there you will have beast side by side eating, beast.

The table of God that is prepared before you in the presence of your enemies is clean of any beast. The food adorned with His fruit is its honor and reward. I say unto you: celebrate in My name in joy, but beware of entertainment in My name, for entertainment is for self-exalting and enterprise. I am neither.

I ask you this: Has God made a game of His Word? No. Does God amuse Himself by being the entertainer? No. Does He make you a puppet when you come to Him praying for His forgiveness? No! God is not mockery. You receive His love freely.

God does play music and He does sing, but it is from the Spirit of Fruit that He does so, and nowhere in the Spirit does He ask you to pray any other way than with an open heart, soul, and mind… in awe and reverence of His glory. For that you receive His gift of love. When you seek to entertain in My name, go be the entertainer and when the curtain drops, take your bows and go out with the act. Play in My name, be like a child would be, in full wonder of God. But woe to you, if gaming to your benefit in My name is your deed. Let not your mockery be done before God, and what is a game to be over another…will turn false in His eyes. Love is the fullness of His glory, and the fullness of His covenant with you exalts glory to glory in His love. Abraham's

Covenant was a fullness of prosperity and love; it was not an act of entertainment. I gave life, land, and fullness to his faith.

As a human being, all of you are all children under God. You who exalt yourself on high in My name for your advantage, woe to you; for My name is not over anyone in heaven, but beneath them I rise on high, lifting them up to God. My name is above all names, because it raises all up to God, who is above all.

I am the first morning star. I serve all others by being in God. You who seek esteem in your name and in My name, I say to you that you have your heaven. For you have been given a place of glory whosoever believes in Me. But you, who are raised on high by God, in your own name and in My name are given God's glory forever and ever. And those of you meaning to do well in My name, but not at the cost of their own glory for another… I say to them: you will be the last to make it to heaven and only after you have shown well before God. You must pray and remain humble in God's glory and a servant to all those who need to be saved. For when I return I will be hard on rock, and the rock will shatter that which does not heed to God.

Can you hear sound, or is it the vibration and the hearing that occurs from those waves? I say not by sound alone…for God is even more than the sound of his Word. God is more than the vibration or the wave. Such as, when you hear the sounding of the sea by its waves, you can also witness the movement of a large body of water, I say God moves this way. Serve only man, and you neglect God. Serve only God. By so doing you will surely serve man. Neglect your fellow man and God will serve you His wrath. For God put you with others to serve and behold… this is the way a wave works its way through! God works through you when you are in service. And be of the sea, both the body of water and the sounding of its motion, both fellowship with God and others, and you will be given by His glory in My name

Jesus Christ…a fullness, and a balance on earth as it is in heaven. Stay in faith and be healed. Stay in faith and prosper. Stay in faith and receive eternal life. I tell you the truth: what is of God is revealed as you come closer to God. What is hidden from you is nothing. What is revealed is God's love when you seek Him. The leaf and the flower are of this season and new birth is given in the next season, but unlike either leaf or flower, when you seek God, you will not subside to a final rest. You will always be God's birth, renewed in God's glory. Know this: the fruit of an apple is sweeter away from the core but more miraculous things come out of the core. And those who ask, "what is God like?" I tell you God is like God. God is like the light of the living water flowing through His Word and branching out to produce fruit, and leaf, and creation itself. Hallowed is the creation He fills, and hallowed is His name, yet I am alive.

To walk in God's love is to be godly. God is all life connected. You wouldn't just worship the life, because out of the life is a new seed to be planted and to be grown. Also, you wouldn't worship the seed or the plant at maturity. You would be in awe from its origination… its birth and all its growth and all its life, but you would only 'worship' the splendor of its maker. You worship God for the joy given you, and the excitement and curiosity of God's given glory. You praise God out of inspired awe and fear. You are more like God when you are a child who peels away an acorn to the seed and sees the value of the acorn in all its splendor and all the possibilities of that seed's new birth. The seed's birth is more like God. But it is the creation of the seed that leads you to God. Seek the creation by the Word, and God will be beside you. Your growing faith in My name, Jesus Christ, is to be like God. God is like your will when your will is aligned with God's will, and glory be to God… watch for the moment of God's glory in you, and His glory is a continuance of His new birth. Also because God's will is all powerful and anything is possible, then what is not, "is", when God enters back in. Now believe, and call on Me to hear the sound of your God. For God will sound a healing before I come! God will sound prosperity before I come. God will sound a fullness of love before I come. God will sound, while moving over the water, such great vibrations, and for all those who will hear, they will join in song.

"I am the Lord your God and I will prepare you a Garden that will spring forth and feed you while you grow full in My glory. While you grow full in My glory, I will not rest. I will care for you always".

Volume Two: Chapter Two: OUTCOME

I speak to your outcome. Your outcome is that of a believer, in My name, drawing nearer to God, in My name, from glory to glory. Outcome has always been God's will, not your will. God has given you a will and He has given you authority over the earth, and He has given you redemptive rights, so you may enter into heaven. But woe to those who mock God or scoff at His love or defy His gifts; for it still is God's world and not yours, and God does not hear or see those not believing when they come before Him. You who know to pray, but won't, and who don't, are not heard, and not a single word is heard… if you pray without believing. Yet, while you live, God does not give up on you. There is no place in God's plan for anything less than representation of His full glory!

Woe to the believer, who draws close to God but pulls out a golden calf. Woe to the believer, who draws close to God but uses his place with God as an advantage over another. Woe to a believer, who is comforted by his or her salvation and heeds no one else's. For if you stop drawing closer to God, you have put up the wall of Jericho between you and your God. I say, as it has been done, the wall of Jericho tumbled by faith. Now believe, and grow in the direction of God and tumble the walls inside your heart that block you from hearing. Be forward-seeking, when you seek God. The fullness of God's glory is His love for you and that is vast, deep, and true. How great you will be if you give of His love! For what is given is to be given! Those of you who take away your treasures will lose all your treasure. Be true then to God, and all your days will be forward in fullness of His glory and there is no more power in this universe than that of His fullness.

See the seven churches! Make not glass, mortar, wood, and steel, and towering brick edifices, although the labor is blessed. Make My church like water and center on My blood and body as the fullness of God's heart. What is done, is done. What is 'to be' is outcome, and I speak to heaven and earth as My Church. In fellowship, tie to God and flow. His glory is a river and He flows so why shouldn't you. Don't structure God. Man structures His life and builds with those limitations. Man could be more if he didn't hinder himself to and fro. Let God show you how to build with no limitations and make your work a blessing. I tell you the truth...what is a 'light' flows without restrictions. In heaven and in earth, God is the light. Open up your hearts and flow. The power of His glory will overcome in you all obstacles and all structures and all walls. Nothing will stand up against the Word of God. For nothing stands before God that is not love. I am love.

Fear no issue. For God can make right what is not. God is love, joy, health, and glory upon glory. Everything is His glory. He started you in the Garden. So make the world a Garden! Be like the roots! Fill up with the rains of His glory. Raise up to the sun and become a strong healthy willow. Raise up to God and create the healthy willow.

In your prayer, you ask Me how to overcome the issues of your day. By faith. But don't fear the issues that flow out of you… fear only God. God has the power and the glory, and God is a loving God. And God loves you. Fear this, if you are part of an issue that lessens God in any way, then you are less in His eyes. If you are a tree with no roots, you will die.

It is neither the seed, nor the plant bearing fruit, that you should worship. Worship only God. Worship what God has created by His Spirit from birth to fullness and then renewed. Your issues, by your acts, without the will of God are yours, and not God's.

Your acts are yours, and God has given you authority over your own acts. If they are not God's, then repent and steer straight to God's Word. God is wisdom. You are not God, so you will fall. Draw on faith that you can rise again! Draw on the issues of life from God and seek His kingdom, and all of life will be added on to you. Become a nation of hospitality and fellowship. Share the 'good news' and share in the goodness of His heart. Fill your hearts up with God's love and move mountains. Open your eyes and see God moving on the earth in fullness, and over waters, and on high above. Bow and praise God for your blessing here on earth, that you may live and breathe, and share with others the power of God's love for you. Let it be known, it is not God's will to destroy the world. Did God not tell you, that he would not forsake you ever again, but lift you up to His kingdom?

Believe! And it will be so. So, what harms you is unguided. Look inside of yourself to Me, for the answer to bring your issue before God is My strength. You are made strong by My strength. I speak to you as the One who defeated the devil for you, but still it is you who must overcome Satan. Satan has to do very little, for many of you are on course with death and destruction. Only man can take authority over the devil and seek the will of God. Don't be the lemming who jumps over the cliff and abandons life, not knowing why. God reveals and nothing is hidden, if you pray believing with a pure heart. I tell you the truth: misled believers will follow non-believers and not know why. Once you seek anything that is not God, you seek your end and become lost as to what and whom you seek.

Go forward in God's glory and receive God's glory. The power of God is yours now! You can have all that God has promised. You only are asked to love God and love your neighbor as you would be loved, and for that, you receive God's eternal glory. If you are deaf, you will hear. If you are blind you will see. If you have an affliction, it can be cast upon the cross and trouble Satan's day not yours.

Volume Two: Chapter three: SURRENDER.

Give to God, and what you create is holy. The battle for God is fought, when you can surrender what is Satan's unto Satan. Take authority over the earth, in My name Jesus, by putting on the armor of God and by seeking God from glory to glory; put Satan under your feet as a footstool. Don't prophesy worry, or horror, or failure, or doom. Wash the sin from your hearts. Only surrender your love to God. Don't make the practice of sin, a life. But I say, fear only the Lord from your reverent heart. Let the Holy Ghost lead you to a place where your sins can be washed away. Let those bonds that Satan has on you; go. But with God's speed, pick up the reins of God. Find the way, in My name and continue to find in your heart, the glory that makes this so. Take the spirit of fruit into battle and clear a path for God. Your heavenly body is of His light and light you will be forever in the path of His glory. You will be from one end to the next and all-between 'knowing'...

from beginning to end. Those who come to His kingdom will hear Him and be cleansed, and washed renewed.

Surrender and become. Give and receive. Love and know the Lord loves you. For to surrender love unto God, is to 'become', and with God, nothing is impossible and what you pray, you receive as it has been told. What is given when you surrender, is the surrender of God's kingdom and all the love God spoke when He made heaven, earth and you. God gives you your right to His love. Fill every fiber of your being with His love and you will be made whole. You will receive love abundantly. God surrenders what is God's to you as you draw closer. You need no signs or miracles, although both will flow nearer and nearer as you draw closer. You only need faith. Pray, believing the will of God, and all within the kingdom of God and more will be added to your name. The fullness, that is your right to inherit, is the emergence of His Word. Seek the Word of God for guidance.

Surrender your faith to God and all the days of your life will bear fruit. The real fruit, however, is in the Garden and it grows for you in your place, waiting as it ripens for you to have. You can come and go in the holy flesh. You can see one another or not. But always, God will be with you. Surrender all that you have of this world to God, and receive all of what God has planned for you. Give and you shall receive. Love, and you will receive the glory of God's love. Share the Word and your spirit will be filled, and you will not want or perish. Remember this, it is the core of the fruit that bears the miraculous. It is from seeds that life spring forth, and not from the flesh of the apple. It is the heart of the seed that holds all the mystery to life. I will come not to fulfill the prophecy of Revelations, but I will come so that you may raise up to your Heavenly Father… and yet the prophecy will be honored. I will come to do God's will by God's will, and judge those filled with Satan or dead to God. I will restore the world not for your sake, but for God's sake, so that God can roam the world with His earthly creations.

It is God I serve in all His works. I will never leave you or forsake you as it has been promised. Hear Me now, if you have ears to hear. We will walk with God and you will flow in His presence, for in My name sake, I have earned you a place with God. God serves you, as I am your servant, and all that is asked of you is... to surrender unto Him. Surrender to love, and your faith will allow God to rebirth you the Spirit. I love you and I will not forsake you. The joy of your Lord is your glory, received by your Heavenly Father, and sounded in your name forever and ever.

And this the Lord Jesus said unto me on July 22, 1998: Never forget what I have taught you ... See My heavenly body is all of heaven and earth, and what is stored in heaven in My name is both of heaven and earth. You seek and then tell who you see, what you saw when you heard My footsteps in the Garden. Remember always, the capacity to resist becoming nothing that is in you...is that capacity to resist becoming nothing...in one will...in all things. God is that capacity in all things over nothing. God has overcome 'nothing'. God has overcome Satan. God is everything. Seek God to overcome and be in all things good. For God will overcome, and I will come wearing My full dress.

So, if you want everything to manifest in you a divine moment, pray believing in Me and everything will be revealed to you. For I am the heart of God's glory, and only the heart can reveal all of everything. Your Heavenly Father wants you, when you pray believing, to receive what you call out in His name. Fill with the heavenly rain and fill others with the glory of your Heavenly Father. What is manifested in My name will be. For what is manifested in My name is all good, and all full, and all God. Call down My vision, My glory, My grace, My body, My spirit, My heart, My mind, and take of it only what you need. Do not want, for to want is to never draw close. To need is to come forth and be filled.

I tell you the truth: there is much to be learned by watching the simple things in life. For a bug to live beyond its day, is harder than for you to live beyond this world. Yet, you don't see or even hear, and therefore you never live, but choose to struggle harder than the bug. Not even one day can you live in My kingdom, if you don't know the glory of His Word.

Don't worry that those you judge might not know, for every living thing is given at birth His Word. Still you don't know how this works, or can you comprehend it. I will truly tell you what it is like in His kingdom, so that you will be told again, of your Father's presence. Now behold, see into the water for the likeness of God moving in you. Even so, in one drop, that even if it were one Word…God could fill your cup, and you could drink of that Word both day and night, as if it were the last drop. For you would seek life till the end. Now, if your life was filled with God's water, your life would flow from one expanse to the next and the drop in your heart would be the Word before you and after you. You would live every ripple of His greatness. His power in His glory is to His love, the depth of His grace, your life given to you in the sea of life. Believe Me, God will make a great sea of you. In your sea as you seek His kingdom, you will live an abundant life made whole, and all will be a living sea around you, living in harmony. This is the kingdom of God.

But woe to you, or any man or woman, who sails the sea and drifts. For you will drift over the truth and never know of it. I tell you, the 'truth' is like a ship not bonded to the water, but rather it floats on top of the surface and moves on His light, knowing nothing of what is beneath the surface, but truly everything beneath and above the surface is God's creation. And what is beneath the surface is hidden to the passerby, but it is revealed to the one in the light of the Father.

Beneath the surface is great depth yet in submerging yourself in God there is no limit to His depth; you will see the drop of water in God, and a sea in you, even as you stay afloat. The whole sea of God is His full heart of love in you. So when you submerge yourself in My name, be baptized and fill with the spirited living water from the great depth of God's love. Fill from below and all the way to the surface, and what is above the surface into the great vastness of God wonders. For you were made out of His image to sail the seven seas of heaven and know their depth, and it is out of His image that you live to know His depth. Love is greater than even this, in His truth.

So, where you are empty, image God, and be filled. Now, let us go forward in the favor of the Father and in My name, and make of this world the Word…His Word…love. For what is love? love is God. The Love of God is revealing and you will always find Me there. I am love, in the Father, and all love in the Father's Word, and in My name Jesus, and in the Father, I am love.

I am Yahweh, your Elohim, by your calling what I am…who I am…the only God that ever was, and is, and will ever be. I am that which was the beginning, and that which is the Word. And in the Word is birth upon the land and upon the sea; new love to be and love everlasting. I am the Lord Almighty God, whom you've called El. I am spirited throughout the expanse and in the sound of the Word. From My essential being, I am your creator. I am the creation found in the Word. Seek My Word, and you will be added onto by My Son, who in the Spirit, is My flesh, and by whom, for your sake defeated Satan and gave to you your redemptive rights. I am the Holy Spirit when 'I am' what 'I am' in you…when you pray believing in Jesus, My Son. I am all of the Word and I have made Me, My Son, Jesus, the Word. I am the blood covenant of the Son, and therefore, I am the Son, and I will come, and I will judge you by your unbelief. So pray believing in Me, who is Jesus. For I am God, in all My Heavenly Glory, and there is no God before Me, and there is no God after Me. For what is after Me is gone to you. I begin at the beginning and I begin at the end…for there is no end…only a beginning to all I see and all you hear. For what I see and hear is new birth, even as I am born unto you, so you are born again in Me. For what I am is love. Love is birth and given to life, all life. There is no love that is not birth. All is love over nothing and all evil, and I am all over all things. And what you hear from Me cries out in the Word of God…give all that you have received! What you see and hear is birth, and life, and all you may be able to give is only this. It is all you have to give. But if you seek Me, you will see only new birth, and you will live moving from glory to glory by My love, so that you may give all that you have received to those less fortunate. There is no sound when you travel at God's speed until I, your God, create in you, life. You will live again in life without sin, and then you will hear, and be made whole to see what is in heaven; My heaven is again a Garden on earth. We will begin life again. So it is 'Spoken Word'…

Volume Two: Chapter four: THE HOLY SPIRIT.

"It is God's love that mixes with the rain all through the dough. And I tell you the truth; it is sharing of the "rain bread" that sustains hearts. For the rain falls from the heavens, bonding 'God's bread' to those who share in it." So the Lord said to me who can hear.

"I say unto life and all who hear, your star has touched God's morning star, and all the brilliance of His glory is upon you. Take the 'rain bread' and bless it in My name. Share My life as a fresh rain and all those who eat of it will receive, in fullness, a heart of sustenance in God's glory." So the Lord said to Me who can hear.

"Make of nothing, 'something' in My name… My name; Jesus Christ. What is not, 'is', if it is God's will, you are in Me, who is in Him, who is your Heavenly Father. His heavenly rains pour out joy. From within you His glory reigns. From within you is manna. And called down from Heaven, it is still the manna. But taken from within you, it is the hidden manna. I am the bread of life. I am the manna revealing. It is all there for you, but you cannot go on and sin, for you will not even receive My name. Claim Me alive, My body refreshed with My blood, washed, and brought together before you. And in this way, I am revealed to you in body and in spirit. And when you do, some of you will see Me but not before you hear Me. Some of you will be touched by Me, but not before you call down from heaven the rains. From believing in Me, what is God's will…is revealed. Now go, and become the attributes of God, holy unto your Heavenly Father, and receive the fruit of His labor and be forgiven of your sins." So the Lord said to me who can hear.

"Make the "rain bread" of My blessing and the dough from the earth, in My name, and make of this writing only a writing that so claims the 'rain bread'. I have so blessed this writer, not because he is more special than any of you, but because he hears and believes in Me. Let the labor of this writing be by one, who is alive in Me, and claims Me within the kingdom of God--- and that I am alive, and that who I name to write does hear My truth. Let it be revealing testimony in My name to the process of seeking God and receiving through Me the spirit of revelation, and the gift of receiving in the spirit, and giving in the spirit all the gifts given by God. And let those like a prophet stand in the Word and stand firm to what is brought out by his calling. For it is I who call...And men who I have named today, like Pastor Rocky, although I name many, few accept. My men and women of valor receive My Holy Spirit, for they must give as they will, what is claimed by God... the anointing and the high ground of love and joy. I say to men and women, like those true to growing and cultivating the vine, give what is given in My name, so they may receive. But give the 'rain bread' to those who seek to sustain themselves in My name. My beloved Ken Copeland, along with his wife Gloria, and family, now revealed to you in My spirit, so are those who I have named in each generation, and will continue to call forth. Billy, John, Mary, Martha, or if you be Higgin, or Hagey, Brim, Steward, Graham, Paul, Alan, or Joe, whomsoever---all your names who believe in Me, so I believe in you who seek Me. For I can write in the book of life the volumes of names given unto Me...so you who believe are in My book.

This anointing is for everyone to have and to hold until heavens gate opens. I say to Ken and men like him, and to Gloria and women like her, surrender to God and have what is God's, then surrender unto the people all you can give, give My voice in all things you act upon. Stop famine. Halt war. Make the very nature of child molestation and abandonment cease. Bind Satan, and wrack Satan with all the woes of the world by casting those afflictions of Satan, unto Satan by saying "get now behind thee." Pray to God to perfect your heart. Evil exists in every part of the earth, and when you share the 'rain bread' by praying over it, evil retreats into its shadows, leaving the rain to pour upon the ancient land of your Father. For the 'rain bread' is my manna, from out of my Spirit, and the outpouring of God Almighty's heart. Pray it and I will show you... new flowers will bloom.

The flower of love will be the first to bloom. But know this to be true...My flower will never close for the coming of darkness. It will remain with you always. Darkness will come and grave things will be done by one who is evil. But I will never leave you or forsake you. God will strike Satan down on the hour that Satan is all of Satan. All evil, manifested, will be tossed into the pit of fire, whereby evil will be no more. I tell you the truth: God cannot destroy Satan in His present form without destroying all of you. Satan is intertwined in your lives. But Satan will take a form when you cast Satan out of the remnant. Satan will then try to strike at the Kingdom, but to no outcome. For I will prevail! For 'We' are the light that shines into darkness, and all that is darkness will be in light. Evil will be struck from this world and oblivious to any nature. Tell the good people seeking sustenance, that they have life and all the attributes of God. For this is the good news!

There is no waiting for what is God's. You can have eternal life in Heaven now; in knowing, and in that, receive a higher level of love clothed in joy. Know that you believe and are saved and going to Heaven! You all must overcome your fears and fear only the Lord your God. Faith and love are the life, so have faith in Me for what I have given by the Father. Receive the 'rain bread' and hope for more to bestowed upon you and all. Cast Satan out of your lives. Receive the wet dough and bake the great bread of God, so you may be full and made whole. And for this you will receive a higher love and joy. What is revealed, can only be, by what is overcome. Didn't God tell you that you would receive the latter day rains whereby the Holy Spirit pours out upon the newborn and the old a like?

For now is the day of 'times of refreshing'. Let one, I hear her prayers, pray for you. Let the men who hear Me when I say now...make of the 'rain bread', the Me, on earth and in heaven. For I will, in the spirit, raise the shewbread ten thumbs higher. You will receive God's gifts, miracles and signs, in My name.

I have given a man and his wife, a white stone with their names on it, and now Words revealed for them to give, and by this writing they so give. I ask of you to give the "rain bread" to those who come forth and seek it in My name. I so name more than one, who is to give the 'rain bread' as a food to sustain those who believe in Me as your Savior. There are many others as well, to give of the 'rain bread' as they seek it and partake in it. The names are many, for this generation will grow bread and wash in the rain, and all will be gathered giving My Father thanks.

They now hear and they must claim it so and praise their Heavenly Father. For it is a new gift, yet it has always been revealed. Now, you have the gift to give gifts, like those kings who drew to Me from afar. So given, 'times of refreshing', by My hospitality, the "rain bread" is anointed in Me so long as it is given as God's blessing. It is by prayer in agreement, those seeking to sustain in their faith, that I answer with sustenance. Those who will remain in the glory, now have found their way. They will not want of this world or hunger, but will seek God and all His glory. The rains will pour out health upon those who receive in My name, and many more blessings will be forthcoming. Hear all who share the good news in My name, for there are many more coming to do the Lord's work. Don't exalt them over yourself, but believe what they say, when in the Word of God. Hear, and you will be exalted and lifted in My name to your Heavenly Father's kingdom. All the kingdom is yours for the taking by what you pray in My name believing. And as a blessing, I give the 'rain bread' as sustenance to sustain yourself in the Word.

Now, receive the life and forever remain clean in your hearts and purged from sin. The 'rain bread' is a gift from God, so those hearts may be filled with God's glory and be sustained. The Spirit of God will lead you to the rains, so that you may be strong and take authority over sin. Now, let the bread maker be like the inspired writer, whomsoever believes, and his or her glory is in the work, and his or her heart will be filled with prosperity as well as glory. And make of this bread first, to be blessed as the moving of the Holy Spirit over the earth; claim it for the giving, in My name. And after he who claims the "rain bread" before you, then one who will claim the work given to him, and those who receive of the "rain bread" of the Lord shall give of it, with the grace of God, to those who seek it out. And if whosoever claims it, it is his or hers forever. For the Holy Spirit is leading you to receive the rains from heaven. But I say to those of you those who take of the 'rain bread', you have received the rains and are refreshed. Because of that which I have done for you in the full spirit of My body and the blood of My body…the later day rains will fill up each heart, mind, and soul with grace, and glory. So be it. This will be your joy! Now, it is bestowed upon you by your Heavenly Father." So the Lord said to Me who can hear.

"The only 'why' for all of this, or any of this that ever was or is before us, is God who desires a relationship with you free of sin. God is like a child who wants to play, live and enjoy, but God has never desired to be alone or keep company with the likes of Satan. If you believe in Me, you will battle against evil, and make your God know the measure of your love by believing in Me. For God gave you the gift of life, and the opportunity to live your life given the capacity to resist what is evil and stand up against what is nothing. There comes a time when Satan comes out of his den to ruin the earth, in fear of losing the battle. When Satan comes out, I will come out and face him… face to face. Prepare yourself for battle, for the eyes of the non-believer will only see your death. I see your life, and life you have received through Me. I tell you the truth, the whole world can take of the manna and all of the world will be saved. Then Satan will do battle in the heavenly realm and not the earth. However, the whole world will never take of the manna, because the hard of hearing won't hear. I am the manna that feeds the earth and every living thing. A worm has an easier time of it than one who is in disbelief.

So I say, Satan will come up out of the body of Satan and become Satan whole. Then, Satan will roam. But know this, those of you that are saved before this time will not see this day. So be it. Manna, now go and be a doer, I am your Lord Jesus."

Heard by me who was deaf to the Word for forty years and now I hear.

V2: Chapter five: THE HEART OF GOD

I think you should know what I have been told. For Jesus said repeating His Word, "For God hath not given us the spirit of fear; but of power, and of love, and of a sound mind".

"For God's love is seen in Me, the Son, by all God's grace and glory. And what is promised by God is given in love, by God, so you may know love is the truth. All becomes out of love from being in love. All flows into an open heart. You may give of His love to life. Given in My name for My sake does nothing, but given in My name flowing from your Heavenly Father, opens up the true power of God; and this power is an infinite love. When in love, give of your love unconditionally to any and all. For such love, will repay you while you live, and much will be added onto you here on earth and in heaven. For God so cherished life...so it is your life God brings to the full. For what is love and what is life is the heart of God. Cherish God for love and life, and God will draw close. Whomsoever goes the way of God's love will go the way of God's heart. I am Jesus, the heart of God. So go forth in the Father as a spring of fresh water flowing freely. Go...that you may flow through the heart and be made whole! Flow and be cleansed. You will hear the Word if you do this, and you will know that it is not the Father, nor I, that said suffer, or die. But take of God's drink, "Eleeo Murizo Sikera", and live in love forever. For your works will be great and astounding to all. God will work with you always. I tell you the truth: Only when you are in the cycle of His love...love of the Father, love for one another, and love returned to the Father...can you receive the gift of His true power. For God has given all. For God has poured out through Me and unto you, the power to be God's love. I tell you this: have faith in what I say, do what is good, and become good and all God's love will flow through your heart and into My cup. I will drink of your goodness in God and the Father will know you by your heart. Your power will grow unconditionally, and many splendid and great things will happen for life on the earth because you did this and acted on it. I say to whomsoever hears God's love... 'say it' and it will be so. As your heart opens, so it is the sound of God's love and now you can hear.

You shall know, I am in God's glory; an ageless love of everlasting spiritual youth. I am the blood of the Father's heart. A love like this, an everlasting love, heals all wounds. What is made whole--- is filled by the Spirit of Truth. And of God's love, I am made complete. 'I am' that 'I am' in God's love. So shall you be, when you seek the glory of God. Say to God when you come "El ja na yada yada mana la aster purietos stereos jel mana mana e ai na Christa Kurios agapeos tekias na na mana osea sana sanna say." For God, this is bonding My love in the Lord for you and all.

Why do you not come?

Why do you still not believe?

For I was lifted up from the earth to draw all to Myself. As for the person who hears My Words but who does not keep them, I do not judge. For I did not come before to judge the world... but to save it. I did not come that you would become a religion.

I came that you could be free to have a relationship with God and be free. Still, you make of your beliefs a golden calf. It is not one belief over another, but glory to glory; one on one with your Heavenly Father. Yes! Fellowship and love one another. Share the good news that you are free to worship God and challenge staying in God by believing in His Word.

I laid down My life for the sheep as a good shepherd. I am God, as God has given Me birth in Him. He has graced you all who believe in Me with the Holy Spirit. Such a gift! Yet, such hardened hearts of granite...for there are more of you who shut the door to heaven than open it up. For you will not believe what is told and what is shown. So then, by Me you've been told and shown. By your way of thinking, so you can accept your Father's plan, know it is Me who comes to save My Church. Take up what has been given. I am the light of this world. I am the light of life. See the life in the grass, the trees, the birds and yes, in you. Do not be amazed that all those in their graves will hear God and come out. All will hear the truth. I died for all of you, so you could be free of your sin. Those who have faith will rise to live. God is spirit and His worshippers must worship in spirit and in truth, what is God. God is the living water, and those who seek a relationship with God will know Me as themselves; for I only serve God. And they who serve God will draw from Me the light. God is more than all the religion in the world and throughout the universe. God is more than all the life in the world and all the life in the universe. God is more than all of Heaven and earth. Yet, you are written in God's Book of Life, if only you believe in the Father. I am of the Father, so believe in Me. But don't make of Me silver or gold. Make of Me a way by which you come before the Father. Through Me, the Father showed you how to approach your own life and your own relationship with God. Why do you make what has been shown to you your non-belief?

When I said you could only get to the Father through Me the Son, I meant I am beyond the crossroads of all paths leading to heaven's gate. I am the path of glory to God that narrows at the towering gate. The gate will not open without the key. I am the key to the gate and all who come must make their final choice. It is not a religious choice. It is a spiritual choice in God Almighty. You either walk with Me or you walk off the path. Stay the course, be in right-standing with God, in love, and in My name. For My name was the Word spoken by God that created the heavens and the earth, and all the universe. All those who seek God, must seek My name, Jesus. I have not lost one. For those worshipping God, all choose the clear living water and God's cleansing. All tribes and all races come who seek God. By their belief, they are on God's path. By conviction of goodness, and righteousness they come. I greet them and show them the way. But those who do not believe in God or seek a relationship with God while they live, never see a thing of Heaven. I will not even extend My hand. For nothing of evil gets a chance with God. No one comes before God, who does not believe in God as the Father. All who come will be raised up in the Father's name. No belief that is false enters into heaven. But I tell you the truth: God is honored by worship and God will honor whatever path you are on, when you first come before the Father.

It has never been about any one religion. It has always been about freely worshipping and loving God your Father. Make of your beliefs not a religion, but make the Father the center of your love. You are less by casting your love on your adornments. Christians believe in Me who I am. There are many Christians who don't know who I am and practice being Christians for other reasons. I am who I say I am, and I am your Lord Jesus. I want you to have your own relationship with God as do others, pure in their nature for God; do this by heart. I am a friend, who came to make more friends, but no greater than your Heavenly

Father's friendship for you. Don't give up on loving all walks of life and all who walk in life toward God. I am not the only Holy Host, for God draws dear and near to all who seek God's glory. I serve all who come into God's glory and I am served by God. Now pick up your mat and walk toward God, and all of this that is the Word of God will be made clear.

V2: Chapter six: LOVE

Jesus spoke to me and said, "If you won't stand for the love of God, then what will you fall for?

If you cannot bow before Me, then how do you expect God to serve you. For God will bow down to a man or woman of His heart. A heart full of God means nothing more than an open heart full of love for God. But if God is not there, then sin is there; even though you are capable of your love, your love will hate and this is not God's love. Your love alone, without God, cannot win over Satan. Only with the love that God has given you, can you win over your own evil and over Satan. Only God's love can win over the sin of man. Only man can take the authority away from Satan and win over Satan. God gives you all the love to claim a sinless remnant and a land full of light. Yet, you profess to love without God. This is like a flower that grew tall and wondrous, and yet the first wind uprooted her, roots and all, while other nearby flowers remained planted. And the flowers beauty soon perished because it was left by the wind to die on top of the ground. So the flower perished, and those of you who seek your own glory will die this way. Even though, close to the flower's exposed roots, it rained, and the rain went into the soil, and the soil was the most fertile in all Israel, still the flower could do nothing to survive. But you who choose to believe in Me, can wash in the rain and gather up in the fertile soil, and root in God, and survive in His beauty forever, by seeking My love and glory.

You cannot profess to know a thing without the Word of God. The attributes of God's love are in My name...the name of Jesus. The universe was created into being by My name, for spoken, it claims all for all, who hear the Word in My name. Call My name on top of the mountain and it will fall unto the land. It will raise the dead, and spring forth the life, and give to you, for your effort, such joy, that the heavens will open up and the rains will pour down. For then your roots are deep and you'll resist the wind to its full measure. Even if your flower is ripped away and the stalk is broken off to the ground, the next season you will grow from the bulb. Satan will be defeated by you!

Yet still, you profess to know what is real about the universe...lots and lots of things you reply. Yet still, you tell Me you are more real than God. I tell you the truth: only one thing is real and this is God. You say, however, you are not God, but you are real. You are made real to God, in My name. You are nothing without God. It is true God is not all things; God is not sin. God is all things not evil. If you are real as sin, I don't know you. Be gone from My sight!

God is all things over sin. Sin is nothing to God, yet a man can be made sin. I was made to be sin, made sin before all. I took all the sin of the land and bought your right to be standing in love with the Lord your God. I redeemed you from sin. Sin is not made real by God, although it exists. It is the work of Satan. It is real to Satan. By him your birth slows to death, and only a relationship with God can save you. So if you live by sin, then you are very real to Satan and you will go the way of Satan. You are either alive unto God, or alive unto Satan. The choice is yours. Alive unto Satan is certain doom. Even as you live following Satan, you will die corrupt.

God is renewal and birth, in love, creating the moment. A man in sin is destruction and will perish in evil. Remember this My children; God is all things not sin. When you sin, you fall from God's grace. Woe to you if you do, for what is real is your sinful nature and this made over a life (the very gift God gave you), makes nothing, and is nothing to God. Your life is spent in vain. Your sin is useless to God.

You should be aware that God is real… made in all things of God, for God is love. God is the universal 'real thing'. The 'real thing' is passion and birth for creation. It is in man and woman, babe and beast, life and eternity, that God seeks a relationship with you. God touches the bottom of the sea and extends to the top of the highest mountain and beyond into the vast expanse of the universe and Heaven. For God is the moment that good conquers all evil. In any moment where God is, all things are possible unto life.

What are the shape and forms to come?

Why would I come and to whom, and not come to all?

Yet, I say unto you that I have come to one who lets Me. When I come by My Father's will, I come in His glory, and a new beginning is made. Your will is free of mine, so I come to those who know it is I the glory. Through those of you who understand, I prepare the way for you to see Me, by those who believe in Me. I ask only that you have faith, and I will appear again before the end. By His will I come to restore even the small things unjust, and make justice of His will to reign upon His earth. I will touch you with love so complete, that even as your faith is strong and on the path of glory, it will be glorified in heaven as love whole to all. I will heal all wounds, and you will talk with God, and your heart will be given over to His glory, and by grace you will receive the power of your God. You will celebrate and share the joy with all His children, and you will love even the farthest corner of His light in another being, creature, and living thing. For what crawls in heaven is alive in God.

Surely your life has led you here…to now, to the moment, to the promised land. Yet still, I weep for Israel. It is hard to hear against the wind and the mute sand. For you cannot hear the quietness of sand, or when the wind fills your ears. Some are not deaf, but act out being hard of hearing. Some are deaf, but they can be made whole to hear. But some are deaf because they want to be. Woe to the 'want to be', who claim being deaf, for they hear nothing of God's music in them and God's music is the sounding out of the entire spectrum of his glory. No stream or thunder or rain is ever heard of the ones who chose not to hear. Say My name to them and hearing will come. The worst of you are the hard of hearing. You choose only to hear so much and then not at all. You want to hear only what sounds good. I say unto you, the sound of God is beautiful in its roar and yet, none shout His name from hilltop to valley, for the roar hurts their ears. The full roar of God is His truth, and such truth is sweeter than your life without God. But you don't believe it. You want to sin just a little, to indulge just so much, and ignore the sounding that it is 'all God or all nothing'. You cannot have both God and sinful pleasure. Where is your belief in God, that you would not believe this to be so?

You tell Me all is well; clothes are better, food is abundant, shelter is ample, and you have the faith! You claim it will get better 'only if'…Poor Israel, poor sweet land of false hopes and dreams. It is 'all God or nothing'! For worse or for better, I say this to you, heighten your glory and prepare the bride for marriage. Be of ample heart and then I will believe in you being better. Yet, you pray not to Me, but to God only, and I am the one who hears for God. Moses told you about God's glory. Those whosoever hear,

'I am', Abba's heart of glory in you who believe. Those who hear', I will manifest all Israel as one land on earth. Wait and you wait alone letting time go by as you bury your dead. I tell you the truth; a better world never comes with lack of faith. What comes is a haunt of your ambition…to make a world for 'self' and not by the will of God. God has intended more for you than your own imaginations. God intends His will be done and the unfolding of His plan. Draw closer to God and God will draw closer to you, and only through Me can you draw close; for I died so that you could be reborn and be delivered, and I was resurrected by Him, so you could be alive in Him. You are born this day who believe in Me, for I have taken away all your sin. In all your glory, you cannot sever sin from your heart if you do not believe in Me. And truly what is sin, is not better, but worse in death.

God unfolds the time of your present, but how much better could your present be if you were alive in Me and know His truth. You must first make of your present, the life you live now; make it sinless before God. I tell you the truth: a small bird cannot pick up a large fish. You have no way of knowing how to fish with God. You cannot find God if you want and want. You will receive all the days of your life, an abundance of want and no more. But if you need God then seek Him. Cast your sin behind you and unfold in God's eye, a good heart full of love for God. Then full of the spirit of God… then you who are unworthy will receive an abundance of His love, wanting less and less, and needing more and more. For it is not out of want that you seek God, but rather out of the attributes of God that God has given you. There is no pleasure on earth like the one pleasure of receiving God's grace upon you. Still, you don't know the meaning of His Word. You are not made better for seeking God if you are lukewarm in your belief. For God is the creation of the His energy and power, and the creation of its dust into life. Seek God from your position in life. For you are men, so stand as a man. You are women so stand as one. Neither woman nor man is beneath one or the other in life, but they are higher in life, in God's own eyes, if they believe in Him. But if they don't, they truly are low, and God did not make a low image of Himself in them. Beware of the mirrors and tricks of Satan!

Hear God before you claim that you have it good. It is not good to be poor, hungry, and starving. Even as you feed yourselves, you stay hungry. You do this to yourself. Your thirst cannot be quenched if you drink with Satan or the company of one with a false vision. Your Messiah has come and now is here, waiting as I am, on you to seek God. I will come and fill your cup, you shall never go thirsty. Our Father only knows when I come, but I wait with you to hear you call My name above all names. For what is in a name? God spoke My name and the entire universe was created. The day will come when the sinless remnant will see Me appear. That day you will hear My name from the voice of God. Tho hallowed be His name, it is I who name you deaf who cannot hear, and it is I who pray that you will hear.

Now as for the poor, starving, and truly hungry, give all you can to them. It is not good to shackle the poor and live without them. It is not good to war on the land for naught, nor reason. God is intending you to have an abundance of God's love and this is better, and this is only sustained in His glory. For love is whole of all that God is. To be on the path of glory you must draw closer to God and walk in God's love. This is hard for you to do, because you do not believe you can be fed, clothed, and sheltered in this way. And yet, time and time again God has shown Himself to you, and time and time again, God has fed the whole nation. But still, you don't believe. You don't see God working in your life. You are hard and it is that hard rock that I will shatter when I come...when I come.

What is in your life is not in another, but what is there is God.

For you are unique and different. So, it is with God...different for you who are of this world. When you sin, God flees and you are left vacant as a haunt.

I came and spoke, and much was written down for you to read and learn of My Father's way. Now I come, and I write as I speak, by a voice that my messenger can hear. Would it matter if I come to take your will away?

I am not your will. And there are those of you who will not take up with Me in My Father's house. I can do nothing against your will. Only the Father can. He will send Me for Glory and for justice. If your will is aligned to His, you will be made in His glory. If your will is made over to the master of trickery, your will is separate from us, and you will go a separate way. That way is death. By such truth told to you, so it is still the same this day. I write all I can this time, so nothing is broken, and nothing is missing. Life or death...you choose.

But always, for any of us, it is the same God...God is there in each moment, never will God leave you nor forsake you. And it is the same for Me. So bring forth from the rain and the soil; from God's future plan, your bloom, your better world. And this I will uphold. Do this and be firmly planted when I come...when I come. For if you are truly of God, you will bloom forever and I will tend to your nourishment. My Words are life to your flesh.

For the power of God is His gift in you. I tell you the truth: God is not sin and true power is God. Sin is death and the power of life is life. What comes from, or goes forward into the future night, is God. But you do not know this to be God, because you bring sin into His world, and even though you pray to be sinless, you must loose your sin to the cross. You who are evil, will never loose your sin, but harbor it until the day your flesh rots. And it is you who partake in sin that cannot see the shape and form of God. For you who sin, the shape and form are altered and they are not the issues of God, but the state of evil. God does not dwell where sin overcomes. But what is everlasting in God? God's power. And those who seek God and those who follow in the Word of God will receive all of the power and the glory as I have. I am the sinless remnant, along with you who believe. I am before you and I am in God. No sin will pass before Me. Remain in the sinless remnant and God will house you forever in His secret place. On high you must come to be included in God's plan.

So, come My children and cast your sin onto the cross. Let Satan die His final death. It is time God reigns and you share in the treasures of the Lord. For I have been given so much to give and share that I can fill your cup forever. I will say no more than this until I come and when I come. God gives power to the sinless and goodhearted who are filled with the spirit of truth, and this is the final truth throughout the entire land. Seek the power of God in love and all will be better. In God's time I will come and the light will scatter the darkness and inflame the hidden sanctuary of Satan. Be ready, for I will come. You have all the opportunities to be real with God and come before His eyes... worthy of His glory, His power, and His love. So be it!

From out of the spirit are all things made physical. But only what is God-given can be filled with the spirit. So if all is given by God, then all can receive the Spirit. You have only to ask and receive in My name, Jesus. Now go in the continence of God, adding no more than what is God, and giving all that is His to those in need. Go give to the non-believer, and stay in love, share the good news, for it has always been good and made whole by the Word of God. I have arrived to fulfill the scriptures and declare the day is His outpouring. Celebrate it with the good news.

Go not for you and your own continence, for you will be like flesh and lose your usefulness. But go forth like the rain that falls from the clouds and you will be lifted up again in a cloud. Fear no man. Fear no ambition. What is revealed to you is God unfolding His plan. And what is God is good. Know this: it is not man inventing the wheel. God's plan reveals no man's ambition. A man is what he accomplishes seeking God. And what God has given He can take it away, but a man can never take away his sin without God's forgiveness".

VOLUME 2: CHAPTER SEVEN: SPIRIT FILLED

My heart is in Jesus and this is what I heard.

"In this world, without Me as your shepherd, there is no way before us than those things against us…sin is his (Satan's) weave. So then, put on the armor of God and deliver God's Word unto those who will hear, protecting the Word of God from him who is in the world. Now prepare!

Know this: you cannot put expectant life on hold, nor should you take that life at anytime, nor expect that life to wait once it is born, for birth of life is precious and sacred to your Lord. I go before the Father to free life in the bounty of His grace. Your Father's will is all things in love. For what is sacred to Me is made Holy at birth. For it is the will of God to give at birth into His realm, a new life.

There is only one stance to take in life, love God with all your might and love your neighbor as thyself…by His grace birth is given. What I have said in the Word is His truth. There is not one of you, who did not come from God's plan. All of you are to be children of God. Yet, as you stand before God you are tempted, even snarled by Satan. This is not God's plan for you, but because of sin you are put out from God's Garden. You exist among the evil ways of sin. But Satan should not rule the world, you should. Although, at times you allow Satan to be the ruler …it is still God's world, His will and His plan. Be careful whom you give the world up to, for I have claim the meek shall inherit the earth.

It is truth. Still many in this life live in denial, as they deny this Word as truth. Not every battle is won, yet I remain in hope and in Him, the Creator. I have paid your price for you. You can stand in God and be a force against sin, or you can go the way of sin and die your death. God will test your love for Him, but He will never tempt you.

You are tested by your actions and choice. The only request of you by the Father is 'His love be received and honored'. Yet, you love gold before honor. You worship idle time before abeyance of Him. I tell you the truth: Satan is camouflaged in death. You cannot see the motive behind such death. If you turn a rock over you can see what is underneath. If you seek the same of death, you will downturn into the fiery pit, devoured by the gnashing of teeth.

For your God is a living God and death is not His place of dwelling. Now, until the day draws heaven unto earth, be forthright and use your armor that God has given you to defend and protect yourself in God from Satan. For this is to be right-standing in the eyes of your God.

For you are standing to do battle against death, and I for you, and you for Me. We learn love tears down strongholds and builds up people in God. Keep the authority God has given you over the world. Keep it sacred and holy. Keep it in your hands. Keep it in your mouth, keep it in your soul, and in your mind. When you do, you have taken the initiative in faith . For as you flow in the Word, so will you flow in My body. Love and respect all others until they give you reason not to.

Seek higher ground. Be in the wings of God and fly in His glory over death. Each of you born into the world, accountable to life in Me before the Father, are made whole of your pursuit by loving the Father. It is not one, but the magnitude of all...all around the world that pray the Word unto the Father to move and manifest My second coming. There was a man who sought gold all his life and near the end of his life he was awarded gold. Not for the good he did, but because he believed the gold was his. But when he died, the gold stayed above ground and it did not save him. Have faith in God and no other...

Be of joy, for the day will come quickly. And on that day, you who sought your Father through Me will be married to the groom. It is My blood that flowed spirited unto the Father for all of you to be redeemed in His eyes. By His grace, you are given it all...if only you draw unto God and push Satan away...Cast out Satan by standing in God's love. Seek your moment with God. Pledge your devotions and live by the creed given you the day Moses served the ten Commandments.

You must be aware that what you pray in My Name (Jesus), by the Word, is the will of God be done. I tell you the truth: no prayer is answered out of His will that is not believed. No prayer believed by the mind and not by the heart is heard. Only by the heart can God act on your behalf. All prayer that is out of the heart is received. It cannot be anything less than His love. God's heart is love!

Pray as you will and pray as you must, for it is by prayer that you are heard. Yet, it is by worship that you shine through. Your path to God is built before Him by building on love. Your battle is to remove evil from the world. There is no other path to the Father than love. You fill your heart with God and God will fill it with love. Half-hearted good is like drawing up only a half-cup of water, and less, for your thirst will not be satisfied. From a full heart, draw a full cup of water. Point the way to others the cross. I died for everyone, that they may have life. All are equally yoked who come to Me and ask forgiveness of their sin. Truth does not see the colors of prejudice or hatred. God is the true color of light and a unified light has no spectrum. So be it.

God gives you the way to lift your heart up in joy so it may soar! So be it.

Go then! For you must love all, and build out of your walk My trust and love. For many will approach you with gloom and sad faces, and they will grow away from you even as they grow with you, and when they leave you barren for Me, don't weep. Also, do not be cold, but know your work has matured in them Godly attributes, and I will call them away to do the work of God Almighty. Incline your ears to hear, for there is much work to be done… There is much before the dawn to finish. There is no land that is untouched, and unmarred by evil. No land was created less in the eyes of the Father, but it is more a bed of coal, fanning him (Satan) in this world, more so today than the fire from heaven.

A woman went to the well to fill her vase with cold water. She thought only of herself, knowing her husband needed water and as well, her children, and her mother and father. She drank her fill. When she returned her father scolded her for not thinking of the others. He loaded her with satchels and vases to retrieve water for the entire tribe. Her shame was so great that she spent three days and three nights filling the water and returning with it. She gave water to each, and her blessing redeemed her in the eyes of every member, for the price was paid in full. Now refreshed, she drank in full measure and regained her high ground and status. So it is true of repentance and redemption in His eyes.

Have a passion for God that ignites a passion in those that are lost. It is the lost, the hard-hearts, and the stiff-necks that need the most work. I cannot standby with anyone who ignores Me, or backslides from Me, or takes to one in idolatry. And yet, I stand for every one of you, even those fallen. For I am here to raise each up to the service of the Father, so you should be devoted to this purpose also. I stand by those who stand by Me, and yet, I will never give up until the day a sinner dies to save his or her soul. For as I have said, 'I will never forsake, not one, who seeks Me'. I have not lost one who turns to Me and remains in truth.

This may be news to you, but it has been so since My time with you: the Spirit of Truth is upon the earth. Such is its power that when you call God to you, you will be filled with such power that your soul climbs all the way to the Heavens and is celebrated at the Gate by your elders.

You have already been won who believe in Me. When you have taken in the Holy Spirit, be of strong faith and let the Spirit lead you. Don't go into the battle without the Holy Spirit at your side and your armor on. My friend in you is a friend to Me, and by the nature of God, you become My friend and we share what is in all His glory.

Walk toward your Father and what steps you take along the way will be counted and measured on your behalf. Walk for God and God's glory. Walk for your church. Walk for the body of the church. Walk and seek out those who will follow you in My name. Walk and claim your building, your fortress, your resources, your tools, and your path. All will be added unto you by the Father, as I have already done for you…for to walk with Me is the very essence of walking in heaven. You cannot come to heaven and expect not to walk. Everyone walks into heaven and into the Garden.

Only God can move through infinity by whenever and wherever. All is witnessed by Us, so make of your deed in our sights good and just. Only God is of the moment all at once. But if your faith grows on earth, your speed becomes relative to that of God's will; stand for Me by walking and sharing and giving and in love, and you will not be still. Walk in love and have it all…deliverance. Battle not for Me, and not for you, but for those who haven't even begun to battle, who are lost, who haven't heard the good news. For as I raise the sword, like you, they will fight next to your side, and they will win such battles as to be counted into one great moment… victory over Satan. In that, My battle will be swift. Your battle will be done. And the battle for Me over Satan will be won one soul at a time. And one step toward God at a time, and I will come to reign one day, complete in victory and glory to those filled with the heart of God, who so gallantly stood in faith for that day. The Father has ordained the return of His Garden. Be forever ready.

What is a white stone with your name on it? It is the hidden manna framed in by God's personal birth. God's birth is given over nothing and existed out of nothing. This doesn't make sense to you. It will in time as you draw nigh unto Me. When God broke the yoke, a white stone hurdled into this universe for each life. It is revealed to you as you seek God. Once you receive a white stone in your name, you are with God always. Forever, that stone is yours and God's. God will keep your stone sacred and inside His temple. The stone is to God… a gem to be kept protected, and it is in heaven that it is harbored. The white stone is kept in His secret place. For God, it is His relationship and your relationship that the stone signifies. To Him, he keeps it close. I am the light of innocence. God attaches a light so great in your name, that its brilliance radiates where ever the light shines. All that it shines into, is yours. All the light from your name on the stone is shining through the entire universe, proclaiming that you are a mighty believer in God. God treasures you more than the stone, but He treasures the light of the stone as a reminder of your love for Him. I am the light of His innocence. When you overcome, God gifts the white stone to you with a revelation that is yours alone. By the honor of God, you are kept close to His throne in this way. Praying, believing, and loving God is how you were given the light from His stone. It is in addition to the light in the Holy Spirit. I tell you the truth: It is all God's light, but God can intensify that light where He may and for what He may. I am not the light of the white stone, but of the light of His cornerstone. The light given you by your Heavenly Father is your light in Him and kept sacred from all. It is this way, so you may have a heavenly body when you come to Heaven. From out of the dust, made of His stone, you are made into greatness before the Father. From the dust he made you in His image, and from the white stone He will make you into His light. Drink of My anointing when His light touches your heart.

For your heavenly body, in heaven, will be as I am. Beware, as not to be the one who blows the light out in the lamp before others have a chance to see, else in the dark one might fall off and you will be accountable for the loss.

All Godly attributes added onto you are measured by your light dress; you by His clothes in heaven, are made to shine . I tell you the truth: all threads in heaven are better than any on earth, yet like earth, there are better threads in heaven. It is by the thread that you are lifted up higher. Still in heaven you can continue to earn the threads of God by drawing closer to Him. He wears the brightest light, and by His gift so do I. I am the light and the Spirit is the keeper of the light. By God's will I delight day and night in His kingdom. Where God directs, I intensify. By your marker; "the white stone", you are manifested in Me, and in your friend, the Holy Spirit. You are resurrected by the Father, for what was given Me is given to you. I am the light of God. By God's will I will give you light. Yet, your light is My light, manifested in Him as you draw the light from within. The light will guide you, protect you, heal you and make alive in you the life here and ever after.

I have never witnessed anyone but Lucifer to whom God has returned to them their white stone. For those whos' stones are in ash, they are not judged until judgment day. Even as a man stirs his ashes, he can have the stone out of the ash, but it is by choice, and he must decide what he believes. Either he will believe his Father or he will serve his death.

But your Father declares to you this day: Satan has his stone and it is death. I have seen other white stones dimmed for another reason…for those of you that heard and turned your back on God. For you, your stone will mark your death on the day of judgment. Be it then, your grave marker that is hurdled at you from Him. Still, you do not hear Me. This is not held close to your heart… for born in ignorance and in sin, you remain… I walk dusting you off from His doorstep. And My tears will pour out on My body.

Too many white stones given that have turned into gray and have never received the light, so I weep…

Do not add to My judgment. They are dim before God. They pile high before Me. Yet, not one of these stones are in the Garden. For you will not receive glory upon glory. So now I give you the light on the Word in this way so that you may continue from glory to glory.

Those that have become ash have fallen on Satan's house. The ash went out with the dusting and shaking of the Lord your God's rug. My burden was great before, but pales to the mound of gray stones nearer to My Garden. Every year I must pick the stones nearer to the soil and toss them to a pile outside of Heaven's Gate. For my angels do this..

None have to be here...so gray and dim. If only you would listen... Israel, the stone, is white and marks everlasting peace. Here is a white stone made out of the cornerstone that you tossed out on the hillside. Again you are given Me, now receive. What Israel will you do with your glory?

Would I be made in His eyes anything less today for I walked amongst you days ago? For if I am anything, I am whatever the Father wants Me to be. In rain I would fall. In the sun, I would shine. In the stars, I would increase. In the heavens, I will be before Him at My throne. For My Father is the Master and without the Master you cannot steer, not even walk, not even crawl. For your Heavenly Father knows where He is going. I see Him in love always. For God is love.

This I testify, your God moves in love with all that He has created. If one thing moves differently, that one thing is left behind from His plan. For all things of God are His love.

So it is with you. Walk in love.

I (Jesus) heard a man speak poorly of his family, how they drag him down and embarrass him of his ways. The sons stay idle and live a life of leisure. The daughters take in lovers. The wife is sitting in her chair ruling the roost, and he complains that he can't get a breath of fresh air, and the respect he so worships. I asked the man what is it that you do? He looked surprised and he said, I do as I want to do. So I asked him, what difference does it matter if your family lives different than you? He told Me they should have respect for him. I told him, I have respected you by listening to you, but still you haven't asked Me My name. Should you show a stranger so little respect?

He said, "Forgive me, but it wasn't me who sought you out."

"But I did you, and you have shown little favor toward Me. If you care so little for your family and none for Me, who cared to listen, then why don't you leave?"

'It is My castle,' he replied.

I replied, "If you are the chicken that laid a bad egg, then it is you who spoiled your own roost."

The man took offense to Me, and scoffed at Me as he turned his back.

I tell you the truth: There are those who will complain until the day they die and do nothing. They will not care to come and seek help in their lives. They'd rather blame their circumstance on the weak to appear strong. But by their own indifference and lack of love, do they cheat themselves. The man can only see through the shallows. I know his family, and they live full and wonderful lives, giving very little of themselves to him in turn for his lack of love for them. The truth is, the man cuts himself away from the family and the love of the family has moved with God. Each family Member comes to church, but for the man. He is too busy complaining.

I have told you anything is possible. But what I haven't told you, is you are not possible and yet you live. By the very stronghold put on you by this world, you can do nothing and yet you think you do. You see your earth in a cosmos of stars, inside galaxies, inside a universe. You see that maybe the universe is dwarfed inside another universe. But you don't know this for sure. Still you think you know what you know. By not dwelling in the spirit and seeking God, you reason to think. The day will come and you will see how little you know… and on that you operate your entire life.

The Spirit knows all that I know and I know all the Father knows, and if you come before Us with your heart, your heart will be filled with all-knowing. I tell you the truth: God only moves into creation and the Spirit fills the creation with God's reality, but it is I who give the reality a name.

If you know My Name, then you know all there is to know. For My name springs forth all the issues of life and on this, and only because of this, can you claim an infinite knowledge and wisdom. God is a force…He is perfection, He is truth, He is His will. And so it is, that we know anything at all. By the Holy Spirit you are filled, but I am a force that binds the very nature of God and the Holy Spirit to you. For I serve God's will. My name is Jesus.

You need to know, but God does not need to know what He already is…God keeps you who believe in Me, and your white stone until the day you die. It is your choice and God's Word.

Yes, the evil one is real. Yes, Satan is on the move. For Satan, the world is his last fortress. Yes! Satan can move off this planet if you do, if you carry sin in your heart. You travel into the big expanse and Satan can harbor his seed in the unsuspecting. How can you travel in space and leave Satan to his demise? You can't. Neither you, nor your fellowship, will be able to stop his move, until I come. To many of you do his work, and keep him in this world. You can pray. By prayer, you can stem the tide. Fight with your prayer work, and live holy. But fight and do not give in to his ways, or his seeds will blossom. Yet, many of you covet even his name. To your way, then it will be, and no pleasure you seek that is sin, will give you a mantle in the house of your God. Surely death will bring you no pleasure. For you will rot for eternity.

The battle is forged by perseverance. Stay in the Word and fear nothing but God. For God will answer Satan in time. It would be better to clean yourself by the Word of God, and all others, before you begin to travel away from earth. Travel you will and travel you must, but be steeped in the Word of God before you do, and even in flight, stay in the Word. Satan is clever to be spread so thin. He is like a virus. He can spread to the four corners of the earth, and he can spread into space as you go from here to there. So long as Satan can touch everyone, I cannot touch him. If I went to destroy him, so I would destroy you who sin, and it is you I have given My life to save. Now you know the truth about Satan. He is around the very throat of the people I love, and have fought to save, and put on the path to worship the Father.

So, it is your battle for Me, and you must do My battle with Me, and we can only tear down his strongholds and push him back where he manifests. It is up to you to do the battle for Me against Satan, until he is made visible by his unification. Then and only then, can I clearly see his ugly body and wage My last attack. You are closer to My coming when the world can have one sinless day. All nations claim peace and love. All peoples claim the earth, and life, and liberty and Me. All who are in the body call Me down, and be not in sin when you do. Call Me into battle. For I will return honor the Father and fulfill the prophecy as it is written. I will strike evil down. I will fulfill the Word of God, and this time the last remnant remaining believes. How I will come has been written, but not when. It is the same, upon God's will, when I appear to the last remnant. Those who remain, I will take your flock and teach them heaven's way. You will not lose one that you speak for. So, know well who you speak for when I come before you and the Father. It is truth: only the pure of heart will come back with Me on the day of judgment. For not even a seed of Satan will pass into heaven.

Know this: if you are half- hearted you are no good to God or yourself, for a heart that has been cut in half stops beating and you will be tossed into the pit of hell's fire. Be a full heart when I come and all will go well for you. Your Father is a loving Father, but He is the highest form of light, and that light will burn sin upon contact. Sin if you must and sin until you are dust, but even dust is burned by God's light when it goes into the spirit. Only a heart seeking God can go into the kingdom. Now you know what it takes, to be a Godly man and a Godly woman who can stand in God and raise Godly children, and live in His kingdom. I will save the person who suffers before God to make good his or her relationship in each circumstance of life, to be complete works of God.

The man who let his mad dog out on his neighbor will be struck down by his lack of faith, for he sent his neighbor harmful intent. And the dog who bites the neighbor is mad, on its own accord, and the animal will follow his master into the pit of hell. But the man who suffered, I will save him to hear his life story. I am certain it will be rich. And he will know Me. So it is for you who treat your sin upon another…

Know this for what it is: it is not 'sex' that is the sin in your life. It is what you lust for and the lust you live for, that tears you apart from all that you are. Sex is sex. But sex done against ones will is sin. Sex is a gift from God: an act to procreate, to give the life you received, in a way that honors the Father. Send love forth into all acts, even what is intimate between you.

Sex, by your very nature is a physical act. For you are born out of the spirit as a physical being. Shared of two will's it is delight and gain. You can love and find great pleasure in the act. This is a sign, that God has given you, the gift of love and creation of your own kind through birth. It isn't the 'beauty in the eye of the beholder' that is wrong by his or her sexual attraction, but it is the eye that does evil with beauty that is torn into pieces and lost. For if your eye is corrupt then so is your heart. That eye that is corrupted before the Father, and by its own pursuit of evil will lead one to blindness, even death. You would be better to cut your eye out, than to look with it and let your heart see the perversion in your mind. Don't fear seeing the opposite sex, or seeing what you yourself would celebrate in joy of another. For joy is life. Fear only if you envision seeing evil or defilement done to yourself or another. And stay in fear if you act on evil. For I will act upon evil and destroy it.

If you like a person and they like you, then it is mutual and it does not defy God. What you do with each other as long as it does not defile your spirit, is the free will God gave you and it is your business. But if you like one who does not like you, and you overtake him or her, then you have committed evil and you will be judged for overpowering one against their will. For God has given every being a free will. If you are the same sex and you love and become one in Him, God will not judge you because you loved each other. God will judge you only if you sin in that relationship, and lust afterward, and commit foul acts upon the innocence of God. You must know this, God made man and woman. He did not make man or woman to defile one another, but to make gain of each other by birth, and by creating compassion. But he also made life for its passion for joy. God made life in you, and you, and you to be joyful. If you are attracted to the same sex, then find your partner in Me, for I am willing; none have sacred rights to Me. Love Me and I will love you. In so doing a man can love a man or a woman a woman but sin is acting in pride to boast the pleasure or bring harm physically to another. I have taken your burden to the cross. As I took all sin upon me the day I was hung. You are free of your sin if you choose to be. I give My love to you. Add My love to your circumstance, and I will love you until the end of time. I will hold you like no other. I will lift you up and exalt you, for you are free in Me to love the Lord your God and all others.

I tell you the truth: It is not a sin to love one another in God. But your own inventions are a sin against God, when by love you worship the act cutoff from God, and not the life of God. It is an offense to defy God by will or by His plan. But like any sinner who indulges, you scoff, for you reason that your sin isn't that bad...you can sin and sin again, until the Day of Judgment. Your battle and wager against sin is no different than any other person. They may judge you, and not even know they sin when they make judgment of you. Sin is your choice, but know this: God gave you His plan. He made both woman and man. The act of respect in sex in both man and woman is born a child. Love for a man or for a woman or man for man or woman for woman in God is love. God is love but God cut out of any relationship is something else. Woe comes from such dead.

Who will stop you, who will save you, why would you ever change from your indulgence?

For the temporal pleasures and the perversion hold you in death, but it is your pleasure. It has been told… the knife in My heart and the stakes that went through Me, and the lance that pierced Me… a torment to the Father, My crucifixion shown you it is still nothing. You suffer very little, but you have a death worse than such suffering when you worship any union by which I am not.

I tell you, no one can judge you this day. Know this: God does not judge you for your love in Me. God judges you for your love of each other, without Me, and those actions before Me without the slightest fear of God. When you worship your sexuality over Me, you have sinned. You defy God's plan who gives to you, be it 'agape', or 'phileo', or 'eleo'. Now, know this: your worship for the same sex is Satan's work of art. You are a cursed but you do not see or know this. It is not your life to walk along with Satan. Seek Me and I will unbind you and free you. Sin itself, has hidden the way God unfolds and now, sin has eroded so much of what was it is no longer a full rich Garden. I tell you the truth: It is not God's work to make sin. What was perfect is not made perfect by sin. The banishment from the Garden resulted in many paths. You are not a woman in a man's body, nor a man in a woman's body, but still you are either man or woman. There is no judgment against you for loving another. Love God first in all your endeavors. To be lovers is not a sin. You walk in God's Garden by faith, love, and by no other.

Only My light heals. You are a man in a man's body and a woman in a woman's body. Have faith that I am telling you the truth. In My light I will surround you and make you whole. Satan cannot touch you in My light. Man is made man and woman made woman and each opposite for each, and each the same unto each in My name and My glory. But none are made for the invention of devices against the Father, that their cause is higher. It is always as the Father commands. You have no rights outside the boundaries of His creations, which are infinite. Beware of what you fight for and what you die for.

Now, you may say biologically you are a different chemistry, and by and large, you have more a woman in you than man or more man than woman. This in these days be true. In the garden it was just man and just woman. The curse came in to the garden and changed the course of events. Even as you are born, you can become a stranger composite than this, or nothing the world has ever known before. For constant living a life in sin will tear down any Garden, and make a desert as it grows weeds. Only in My Spirit can you be made whole of perfect creation, and perfect harmony. By faith, by your relationship with the Father, a love so great… in this, you are made over again in His image.

But I am Spirit! The Spirit of Truth is upon the earth and it is in all life. I am not your mind, nor am I your body, but I am in your heart. When you believe in Me, your heart is set right-standing before God. I will make you whole, whosoever believes in Me and believes in the Father. You are to stand in belief for Me until the day I come and you will be at My wedding. I am the groom and I will make man, woman, babe and life upon life My bride, and she will be a woman before God. And you will witness Me before you that day, as I am the light, and the good herein and in heaven.

This is the day to throw off the shackles and see as a man, and see as a woman, the light within. I take the demon out of your confusion, I make you whole and bring you into your Father's image, made complete. Have faith in Me, and it will go well for you this day. Still, you who choose to be different than your Father's image, and do evil, and go the way of lust, don't seek Me, for I cannot give you understanding, I can give only understanding to those seeking first the Father. I tell you this: All suffering seeking the Father will be restored.

Again, I have cut the chains, and loosened the shackles, but it is you who have to walk away from bondage. I will walk each step with you. Take My hand, and come free. But still you don't understand Me.

I ask you, especially those of you who are woman and man, is your sin a heavier burden than the next sin? Is it any more or less a sin? Take heart… man and woman! What is confused in you is a lie from Satan's own lips! You are made in the image of God for a purpose. And you ask Me what is that? It is your heart for God!! A good heart in the image of God is aligned to His will and you will know no limit to your possibility. You will understand beauty, and in each act where you are intimate, so does beauty become you. Thank only the Father for such good fortune.

I labor this as a good work for you to hear and receive understanding. But you will receive wisdom when you gather before Me.

Your heart is either man or woman. But still you don't understand. In God all things are possible. But nothing is possible without God. For God made man from dust and the woman from the rib of Adam. For what was done spiritually in Us, physically it came to be. There is beauty by each heart to receive.

Now, it is time for you to understand: I will defeat Satan every time, from here and forever more. This day, you have received truth of a thing that matters to you, and so you will receive more, as the day of outpouring comes forth. Understand, you are made as a man and a woman, not by nature, but by God's will. For a man who does not love his woman, or a woman who does not love her man…they have sinned. But any of you who take a child of God who is unwilling, I will come this day and by My power, hand you over to death. It is clear in the Word of God that thirst to harm another, is a sin, and know this: Israel is the land of God across His world, and even beyond to the greater expanse of time and space, but harming another and idolatry are perishable. No sin will remain upon His land when I return.

If you worship your sex more than God, you have committed a sin. I do not look at your sex when you come through the door. I look at your heart! I tell you the truth: The beast of sexuality is named perversion, and it is evil, because it is Satan who partakes in the act of rape, and defilement, and vomiting upon the act of love so endeared to you by your Father. Evil makes no distinction. But what is named 'homosexuals' or 'lesbians' are life, and in God their sins are no greater than yours, and you are worth saving. I came to save your life before God, and it is then as it is now. God made all life, and any life in God is a new creature made whole by His Word. Not unless they cut themselves off from God in disbelief. Beware of your sex acts, for sin is clearly going beyond the will of another. A man who loves another man or a woman who loves another woman, let them love, for God is love. But if they act against one another, violating one another, then they are in sin. Violence is not love. Perversion is not love. Sickness is not love. You cannot give birth by being the same, only God can give birth to His name.

A boy who didn't know better succumbed to sin, but when he prayed to Me to redeem him, in the eyes of the Father, he became the whole of the Father by the Holy Spirit. He loves another man, so be it. Brothers love brothers, and sons love their fathers, and fathers love their sons, and it is whole if they turn to love the woman God made for them. But if you exalt your pride and label and flaunt it before God, you can be sin, and though you love, you love death. Now, go and live, and sin no more.

Do not judge one another---you cannot judge. Even the smallest sin is sin, and by the nature of sin, it can be the slightest offense, yet it is still truly sin. Those who violate God's law are free of your judgment, but you are not free of My judgment, and I will come to make all unjust, just. If you judge their wrong then you have sinned, as if you committed their sin. If a man and a woman are wed and the man rapes his wife, then he has sinned. His sin is sin like any other sin, even though they are opposite sex and wedded. When mankind was made in the image of God, man and woman were pure of heart. Sin has twisted those images into what they are… less than perfect. Still, God's attributes can be found in any living soul, and added onto each as each seek truth in Me. By one or by two they can be made whole. By truth, they can be made whole. By birth, they can be made whole. By sameness, they can be made whole.

So many things in the Word, as God moves, take larger dimensions. It does not mean the purpose of the Word changes, nor does it mean the meaning of the Word changes; it means what is called one thing in the Scriptures is the truth and the truth by His perfection is made whole. But what you call sin and judge by, is not the truth. For it is not up to you to judge. It is up to you, not to sin. Only God can judge. I labor this good work so you will truly understand…

You who call a person, 'an Indian' are guilty of the same thing, for what is native to a land is not an Indian, but still you call them what they are not. What they are is, children of God, and in the eyes of God, His creation. A person with red pigment in their skin is still a person. They are not savage, as you who name them to be such. Every person has a heart, and it is the heart that I see and testify before God Almighty, good or bad.

Know this to be true: God's perfection is far from those things named, for His perfection flows and those things named flow with Him becoming Him. It is from the Father that all things of perfection flow perfection, the Father. The Father adds onto you as you draw unto Him. It is He that gives you those things of Him that you give to love. God does not change, but all things change around Him, as He moves upon them on earth. And all who hear begin to be refreshed. God judges all sin in the end, but even now, your God will show you through His spirit how to take a step at a time toward His glory, and be free of sin. But, if you force yourself onto another you have sinned against God and you will be damned! My horse will cut you with its hoofs. You, who are twisted and perverse, man or woman, or both as one, will be separated from the Garden of life.

Now go into the night and let it be told: the Word of God is truth and the truth lives on in His goodness. Don't get stuck on a page and major in one subject…that is not the living God. Go and seek His goodness in all things made good in Him. For God is awake in all things good, waiting to be discovered by you, and good will spring forth in all things of life, if you let God's will be done. Man in the Son of Man, and woman in the Son of Man. For I am the Son of Man, and the Son of God, and like you who believe, I am a Son, and you are also the sons and daughters of My Father.

Be in spirit, and in union with the Holy Spirit and you will see as God sees. Sin is against the Father when you defy Him. Sin is against the will of another. There are many sins, now more than ever. You are on a great battlefield of sin. It is so available and so tangled in your life that some sin is overlooked, and your heart is entangled by it and strangled because of it. Some sin you don't call sin, because you are the walking dead. I call sin anything that defiles you and another, before the Father. Now, you know what sin is, but still you sin. Pray to God for His Mercy and your soul. When I come, your sin will make the cries and screams of death in the pit and there will be gnashing of teeth, as you follow in like a mad dog. I will silence that scream to the gates of Heaven. Repent now before God, and your pardon before God will be marked. But woe to you… if you continue to live in sin and not know Me. I won't know you that day.

I will come swiftly and quickly. I will be hard on rock and sin. Stay in love and all will go well for you. Sin will perish at the wave of my hand. How fast do I come?…At God's speed and in an instant. How fast can I judge you for your sin? At God's speed and in an instant. So fear not, repent if you need to, and come to a church, and confess. Then pray, and praise and worship your God, and give testimony, as I(Jesus) am your witness."

Volume Three:
ONE WASH ONE SEAM: CHAPTER ONE

For she called it what it was, a seam. God pressed through the fabric, and the veil tore on hidden lies. God was out in the open. And what I saw, was His cross in the shades of His work, by light, you can see His cross. What came was the vision of all is, and all in His name, by the sounding, by His grace, so it is His reign, so it is Him, so all is said that is in the Word.

Then the in firmament again was made whole and all is joined to the kingdom of God Almighty. The mountains roll, the seas roll, the scrolls roll, and universe rolls, and He walks on what is rolled out before Him. All is at His feet to be in Him, called out by God Almighty., "The land of all Israel". I heard His sounding in truth like a roar of a lion. I came to His feet and prayed. He was washed in white light. He, My Father, moved upon a valley and turned and spoke these things: "You would not know that I am. For you don't wish to see or hear the truth. But I am as I am in all aspects of you, as you are in all aspects to Me, one and a vessel of My choice that I have ordained. You in the universe with all things of the Father, are Me. I am your God. I am working forward of you and after you, to do good, and to bring from one moment to the next, the truth. You would not know these things. You have been given many such signs and still most of you pretend in My name. And the most of you don't pretend your death, but you pretend with Me. Stop pretending... for I am not a pretender. I am the living God.

I can give you new beginnings. I can give you new worlds. I can give you love that starts and goes on forever and ever. All things are possible in Me. Can you do this? I know not that you can, or you can and you don't seek with Me that you can. So, you are alone in you and that is your capacity. I am alone when you are alone. I am a lonely God without you… It does not have to be this way; I have such a capacity that between you and I, love conquers all. Love bonds us and love becomes us. Love is the power of all things that I have made. I have such a will. I create it all, from creature to texture, to design to light, to something from nothing, and from Me to you. I do this all to be your friend and take you to places that we may share and care for…such is My love for you.

Would you understand? If I told you one such place was My kingdom … one such place was My temple, one such place was My secret place, one such place was My heaven, one such place was My world, one such place was My garden, one such place was My heart, one such place was My love, one such place was My spirit, one such place was My word, one such place was My earth, and one such place was you, and one such place was Me in you. Now do you know who I am. Now do you believe. Now can you call as I have called to you, My coming. For My love is eternity and this I give to you who comes.

Why have I not come? In God's time and in His will, but I can come to one who can hear and see Me, if he is ordained by the Father to hear and see. You find it difficult to understand Me, as the one who can hear and see, still struggles with his doubt, shaking his head that this is so… yet, I ask of him and he does what I ask. But I have made myself known and you have no more excuses. I have printed myself in the Word. I have moved in the Spirit. I have died on the cross, so you may live. I have built all the processes to sustain you. Yet, you are so bold and so brave and so courageous that you believe only in you. I will not crush you, for Satan will do that if you let him. I will hope and wait. I will love and give. I will create and sound. I will call into the wilderness and call you out. I will never forsake you nor leave you. I will standby you until the end of time. For I have said it, and therefore I am My promise.

Those who believe and have an open heart, are those children whom I bless; they hear and see. They bring Me close in. For them, I expand time in every direction and in every dimension so they may live forever and ever. They walk among you as my sinless remnant. They allow for Me, with what little power they have. For I have all the power and can do so much more; they keep My heart. It is the least I can do to allow for them. And by so doing, I give all a chance to draw to Me: A chance to live. A chance to be heard. A chance to breathe. A chance to reign. A chance to have a relationship with Me, who can give to your chance a new life, worthy of your name.

Can you see by this child, by his will as my vessel, Me? If you cannot you are blind. Lower your eyes on the dust and see among such things as death and all things rotten. Now look at him and see Me. By contrast I hearken things to bring heaven and earth together. Listen to him, who teaches the good news, for after all, he is My vessel. He is laying down in green pastures and filling up with My Spirit as I have commanded.

But if he is so unattractive to you, you vain and wonderful composite, then she is one flesh and one heart, and she is My love and care. See her for your feelings, and she will give to those feelings love and care. But beware, by your composite, you rot before her if you will not listen to her love and go away barren and wasted away. She will mark your death. For my heart is stone to such wondrous composites. She has my heart and she can take the crust and truly make it beautiful. She is of the earth, and when she is not, you will know not another like her. For when I raise My church, she will be gone to earth and reside in heaven. Listen to her, for she who is My vessel in Him who anointed Me, is now among you to teach the Word of God. You might find it in her to pray for you, and you should wait on her prayer with all your conviction. She will not pray for your want, but for your need. I will in a breeze come by you and if I see you've been truly changed, then I will bless you and add to your beauty, and fill your heart with the Spirit. If I come by you, and you are hidden , remaining to be cleaver, you will be baked by the breeze and whither away. Now, this is how I come to know my Garden and what remnant remains.

You would not know this. But still you think you know this and more. What do you know? Can you tell Me what 'txatrite' means? Can you tell Me what 'xexpi' means? Can you tell Me what 'cryptrae' means? Can you tell Me what 'ubewaj' means? And if you can, do they mean anything until I say they do? You claim you know what they mean, and you give them a name and meaning. I knew a man who's pig was his pet, until his hunger got the better of him. Now, what of the pet?

You say you do it all and you do. I drift, and you let Me drift until it is in you to need Me. I am like a genie to you. When it is hard for you, you pray for want and wishes. I did not teach you to pray for want. I taught you to pray to Me for your Father's mercy and forgiveness, that by His will…He would give you His love. Still, you name those things whenever you want in My name that are not the will of the Father, and I cannot but plant them in among other barren rocks.

Those who know Me, however, do not want. I name those things that become and stand the test of time. Your names will go away if they are not the Father's. Like you, those names that are not in Me to name, are not real to His future. I live in the future and know the way. I can bring about the future into your now. You think you go to the future, but you can only go to the moment and not beyond. Yet, I can take you there if you are pure of heart and believe in Me, the Son. For nothing is done without the Son.

I am the Son, and the Son in Me is My Spirit, and the Spirit My Heart, and My Heart is the Truth. But you still don't make the distinction. You discern black from white and so on. I gave you your abilities, not to judge one another, or kill a thing, but to find a way back to My Garden. You only needed to taste the sweet foods of the Garden to know you didn't need to kill to live. But, now you who pretend to know it all. You intimidate others for your own personal glory, who kill for your food, least your time runs out, and you starve to death. And you! You who do worse out of pleasure… be gone from My sight forever. It is I.

Those of you who seek Me, I glorify. Those of you who seek your own glory, I despise. But those of you who live bonded by the commandments, I have more patience and love for your confinement than you do. While you suffer, I wait. While your cry out, I listen. While you struggle, I move. While you seek, I give. While you ponder, I question, for I give you to your need. While you fall, I lift. For I am everything good…and someday you will come to know Me, and I will be there for you.

Yet, there are those who do not cage themselves, and they seek from Me their freedom. I manifest their freedom and give to them a white stone with their name on it. I give them a name and the hidden manna. For they will be all powerful here and now. This is what I give. You wouldn't know this. You wouldn't suspect it. You wouldn't in a million years understand it, but it is I who unveil Myself to you. Yet you think about it, and you argue over it, and like you, you claim it as your idea. I made you, and Satan pulls your strings. I clothed you by your own beautiful skin, and Satan dresses you in clothes of the world. You adorn yourself in such threads, that you are accustomed to the serpent's skin. I find you hiding still in the Garden with your shame. I find you in the Garden this time, not with nature hiding you, but with Satan covering you.

Can you hear My rage sounding out on this. Get free of him and pay your Father with praise for His mercy. Find your price has already been paid by the Son. I have paid in full! But you cuddle with your familiarity and with that which is too good to be true. For this you don't know Me; it is God that you abandon. Satan comes among you to confuse you. You are buried in his feast and not the Lord your God. For God's feast comes as He prepares a table before your enemies. And it is I who come now to do just this, prepare yet another feast to draw you off the pig you eat on.

Now look with Me. This time look with Me. I will show you not signs, although there will be signs. I will show you not miracles, although there will be miracles. I will show you not My gifts, although there will be gifts in abundance, nor My blessings, although blessings pour unto to you who believe, nor My love, for it is always with you, or My heart, of My heart I have shown you and have burned into the Word for you. I will show you Me. I will show you Me. I will show you who I am, to all in the face of evil. I will come and evil will retreat. I will come and by such power in Me, show myself in Him, who is He who created all heaven and earth. When you look upon Me, you will claim Me. I know this to be true. But I will claim only a few.

Some of you will claim Me and then immediately set out to manipulate what you claim. You will be so cleaver and you will exalt yourself to a false high. You will repeat what is in you to play out, for not what was given to you, but by him, the serpent, who will out-trick you. But there will be those who will not stage or act and they will be the new heaven and earth: the love of life. You don't know what heaven and earth is, so don't pretend that you do. Only I know, and I name them the last remnant, the sinless remnant, and they will bring about the way in which I come. Now, let Me tell you what you don't know in words that you know, except the one word, 'heaven and earth'. For the love of life will be in bliss and in joy. In bliss and in joy! In bliss and in joy!

Heaven and earth is the land most sacred and most high. For the earth complete in heaven is the Word, and The Father's sacred Garden. It is, in the Word hidden, but now it is revealed! The land of human and God, washed in heaven and earth, and life is lived in joy. There is no serpent in heaven and earth, allowed to roam on the earth for a thousand years. And then, when he comes in his final form, when heaven falls back onto the earth, the serpent will be made a pit of fire. There is, however, a place sacred in your name for you who make it to the kingdom of God.

Come now that you've seen Me, now come and enjoy. In all life is joy… Build up and build out and grow the land pure and purify the air and the seas. Bring Me alive, and you will be forever sustained. Here is what you will do in My name, "Wash in the love of the Father".

Don't make excuses; don't claim it unto something that it is not. Wash is wash. Wash is to purify. I will sanctify and you will wash. I will purify and you will wash. Wash yourself in the Word. Wash your sin away. Wash your land. Wash the earth. Wash what you build. Wash and clean your heart. Wash away the gutters. Wash the sea. Wash the air. Wash the life given to you. Wash the birds and the bees. Wash the creatures inhabiting this earth with you. Cleanse the whole of earth and you, and wash away the prison. Satan has built you a prison and you accept your cage. For you fear what is evil in you and you cage it. Let loose fear and evil, and give of love and devotion. Now, his evil stronghold cannot stand My love. And no such love can stand evil. So love and then love. When you wash, wash in love. I will wash you with My love. Now do you believe?

Often, like an animal that is not taken care of, you live in your decay. Wash the decay away. Wash all others around you. Wash your cities and your fortresses. Wash everyone and thing with the Word. Wash everyone and thing with the water. Wash every dream and idea with the Spirit. Wash every mountain and every valley. Wash every word in the Word. Wash every notion and every act. Wash your world. Wash as you grow. Wash the pollution away. Wash the toxins away. Wash your food. Wash your heart and mind and soul in the Word. Wash your ambition in My love. Wash what you say. Wash your feet, and His feet, and your neighbor's feet. Wash the sin from the earth. Wash nutrients back into your soil. Wash sin out of your soil. Wash the Word over the earth. Wash Me.

Now, all is washed in joy and bliss and before you. I am your God living again among you in the land of all Israel, the land of heaven and earth.

Do you see it...no more impoverishment, diseases, selfish ambition, hatred, jealousy, killing, weirdness, greed, and falseness? For in this land, all are free of such things. For in this land all are washed of such things. For in this land baseball, tennis, skiing, scuba diving, golfing and every activity of man and woman is played out. But those activities that are killing the planet do away with them or by ingenuity solve the residue of indulgence. For I will lend you My mind if you obey and fulfill My will. For in this land knowledge is light, and the properties of light are pierced, and travel from here to there be played out. From this land, there are no wars. From this land I roam. From this land, I am washed new in you and unfolding I wash you. From this land truth stands. From this land, care and love triumph. From this land, youth glows in young and old. From this land I will come. I will walk. I will wash.

Can you see Me now? When you start to wash in Me what I say, wash and be cleansed. Wash to wash, and you will hear and you will see. You have one chance to wash now, or be wasted…your God will not standby your decay or destruction. Your Heavenly Father will move swiftly to defeat the enemy, and yet there is time for you to prepare the way for victory. Now Go! Hold your head high and be counseled by your Elder.

For My name is everything that glitters in God, from the smallest glitter to the largest glitter you can think of. Life springs forth by adding unto life, and everlasting life is added unto you when you believe in what I have said. Now go, and share what has been anointed unto you, one God, one Heart, one Truth, one Mind, one Spirit, one Soul, and in you there is 'one Will' providing for your free will to be. You are to live life and breathe. Give what you receive and you will have heaven."

Volume Three: Chapter Two
THE 'RAIN BREAD' POURED OUT

I am the servant of the Lord, like those before Me and those now existing and those to come. Hear Him the Lord Jesus. And this is what I received hearing and seeing, as a host of His witness, those in witness who testified, and Him who said these things.

Let your walk be testimony that you witnessed this day in God; Joshua, Moses, I and I Am, and His unity of His creatures, those magnificent beings, and your inclusive heart in those steps we take in the Father. Your children grace even those who know no grace and understand little if when receiving grace. For they are refreshing in My name. So it is with your child that I speak. My name is Joshua, in Him God only. For what He spoke unto Me as Moses, I offer you my gradual understanding. You have shown through by devotion and abeyance, now that you receive of such gifts, as these in the Word of God when you call My name; it will be Jesus.

Upon the very sacrifice given, I say this, so such life lives. I give of this then to Zao and Zeo, and to the wife of Zao such as My love and tolerance, My joy and temperance of their prophecy and teaching of My Word, so in My Father. Keep the Word of God in hand, as I give unto you in your hand. Now, I will talk to you in parables so you will know it is Me, who speaks these words to My Church, and no other.

I ask, would a man discard his wife for pleasure of the spirit if she were spirited and he knew her not to be so. So it will be my command to rise up the first supper hearing the call of hospitality and share the 'Rain Bread' as water to the Garden. Now what gift I give you, go do My work as labor and take not one slice of the work for yourself until you have fulfilled the first supper. Fear not your own hesitation, even though it will take all your confidence to take My servant with you. For even a near perfect diamond is flawed, yet I will perfect such flaws to be rich and many faceted. What is incomplete, I will make whole.

I give of My faith in you as My holy witness each in my anointing, that they will now have understanding that out of the glory His Word is life which pours out the hidden manna. I command to each by My Father's will, His gift complete in His Word, the 'rain bread' of elaia yom manna', the second gift of seven of His unfolding comes as I saw My morning star. Make not one moment, as the sun takes a day, a number, for you cannot count the time of God. Your race is what is given in the breath of life.

Is it not true of how water flows, that by now, the unity of sea and land are pressured by His measure to overcome you with His Glory?

Verily I say unto you, that a woman mistook her husband at night for another. She woke up and not surprised, remained. When the husband came home, he was surprised to see his brother. The husband had been filled with wine and sought refuge away from the gathering. His brother was horrified when he woke in the wife's bed. The brothers did not speak to each other again and hardened their hearts toward each other. She wept and cried out for forgiveness. I lifted her out of misery, and the brothers, I don't even know them. Now, whose sin is perishable and who's sin remains?

So it is of My Church, I will not take in the wreck less, the careless, and those complacent, nor those who stopped seeking truth. My Father is the truth complete. Do not confuse Me with another, for your God is the only God, and there is no other. If you have more than one God surely you will not even know your brother, and if you go to speak, you will not be heard. For the Word of God is written; I am the life.

My Church is not complacent of sin. It rebukes it, and in forgiveness it frees the soul and lifts that soul into My Spirit. You will perish who remain in sin. The brothers who did not speak again the Word, perished. The church remained not to sanctify the act of sin, but to justify what is right- standing in God's eye.

You have heard it said that nothing is hidden, and nothing is missing or broken to those who seek with all their hearts, minds and spirit, His glory, His grace in Us, Our truth, and His will by your will, aligned, then His will be done. His covenant to you, for such as those risen to His heaven by grace, is sanctification in Him with everlasting life in the Glorious place in heaven, the place on high with Me, called Eden. Let it be said that the Morning Star shines upon thy Father as heaven is lit by such power and each day is more not less. So it is, Eden grows more beautiful in heaven each day. As you who have been redeem will come right standing and washed over by His hands, as My own will wash away suffering.

When Jonah was in the belly of the whale, no one sought to search for him in such a place. God knew where he was by his outcome. So you know where God is, and now you have only to search the heart nearest to you to know the heart farthest away in likeness is God working. If you can walk by in retreat of another, and know their suffering, I say your bread will rise no more then the yeast you put into it, and even by each moment sink in retreat as Rome did.

I will look beyond good works for longsuffering. Be made aware of the yeast you make your bread with if you wish to rise. I will right all suffering first and foremost, and those who labor long to suffer with those who are under the rule of Satan; I will rise quickly to the throne of God as My Morning Star breaks through from heaven.

Woe to you who drink My wine, eat of My bread, and take of it without longsuffering and bearing up to the thorns and thistles of such worldly soil. You who know the yeast of your bread and the labor to refine yeast will know My bread is the body of My living Spirit akin to the Spirit of the Father, as one is the same. You will eat of the hidden manna now in heaven.

For I come to fulfill My coming. My Father gives of this early gift in preparation of My way. Like an olive branch before Me, it falls upon you this day. I am as I am, and He bears seven gifts in the days of full measure of My blood. 'Elaia yom manna.'

I heard as I hear, a child was born, not as I was, but as you are and he faced the world like I did, born outside. He suckled on his mother who had little milk for him. His father perished by night. Yet he grew to a child near starvation, and in fear of hunger he ate ungodly things. He acted as a fugitive, but he did not know who the enemy was or even what he did to deserve an enemy. He was told by an old man that what was twisted could not be straightened out. I verily say unto you, he knew that which was against him, was not that which kept him alive. He dropped to his knees and prayed to My Father in heaven, knowing not Me, for I had not been received as yet known by this child, and yet in the eyes of My Father this was holy enough to send Me to him. I tell you this truth: never once, not at birth, or even in the day of being a child did he know My name. The Spirit of My Father found him like Jonah, and breathed into him the life. Now this boy will lead a whole nation to Us. You who know My name can do even more.

I promise you this: each heart who seeks the Father is a child born with wings to travel faster and more complete. Each prayer will be answered complete unto your God's love. Spread your wings up to heaven and fan the very tiding given to you on the hour Rome fell. For of such offering those winds will be your preparation for opposing winds.

I knew a soul who making it to heaven, turned and looked down and said the earth was really nothing. Your Father in heaven sounded and the soul fell into hell. Never before you is it nothing.

Now for all I said, I say unto you so that you will know it is Me: I say, one man knew another by his faith and the man of faith did not know of the other man. They shared the same water but each drank the water by their own lips. One made of the water a stream and a furrow by which he grew seed. The man of faith drank from My anointing and claim My coming. Each man was highly successful believing that I came to redeem them, yet only one shared the others faith.

One day, when each fell from the spirit, the well appeared dry. The man anointed begged Me for more as his thirst increased. The other man sat in the shade of his tree and picked of the fruit he grew and gave thanks. He also prayed to be forgiven and prayed the water would be forthcoming. The thirst of the one man grew until he demanded of God to be given a drink. This only served to grow his thirst. His sheep long ago left him. The thirst drove him over the mountain to the other side and he saw his neighbor and his neighbor's friends in joy. He drew his sword upon them and attacked them with a rage. I tell you the truth, not one of them fell to his sword. Woe to whosoever draws My waters and drinks of My anointing for gain and power over my brothers or sisters, even those not yet drawn to water. For in My anointing, life is between a man's abuse, and his self-inflicted wound, and one who seeks in faith, My grace. I will walk by you and not know your name even as you once were anointed, if you worship the anointing over My Father, it will leave you barren.

Make way, for the river will part and the meek will walk over into the Garden, the holy land, the place where they will inherit all God. Come, all who can come. Come, that you may walk in heavenly ways.

I know many who walk, but they walk in earthly ways claiming My Word will bring forth wealth and rich strands of gold, silver, and pearls upon jewels. They even adorn the wealth given them calling it prosperity found in the secret place. God has an abundance of wealth for you in heaven, but not of your understanding. A man wore the finest dress, and he wore pure gold. He sent out the Word of God and touched millions and by the Word of God he saved millions of souls. He gave of the wealth given unto him in My name. He hears from Me as I receive his prayers. But he does not receive My prayer. What does it gain a man if he gains the whole world and nothing of heaven? You know who you are, now release all of it to labor. Till the soil and raise the heads of babes in distress. Build out God by the Word of God and no other.

Wealth in heaven is a constant stream, a torrent! It flows! It never ceases, and it is God. This is My offering of the 'rain bread'; take only the wealth of His Word into life and not your purpose.

I tell you this: My holiness is not judged, so why judge your measure above mine. My purpose is to bring forth salvation, and by justification you are made right-standing in the eyes of Elohim.

Comfort is only in the Word of God and it is life. You wear My crown and only He, My Father, makes it. Only by His grace, can you wear such fine richness beyond earthly treasures. Now go and give the crown of glory as it has been given unto you and I will wash your feet. Woe to the one who has stored up the wealth of many nations, and in the street a child is being consumed. I will come, not out of vengeance or sense of revenge or wrath, but out of justice and you will be consumed by hell's fires to be in death always, written as nothing to your name.

My grace comes to those, who in faith, plan for more faith, so they will be carried in troubled times. Now know this, the 'rain bread' received pours out the hidden manna. I 'elaia yom manna'. Revealed, it is My preparing for His vision, your Father who brought in the Morning Star will do so again. I will come as I am called, and as you prepare with the Father and the Holy Ghost… didn't I say I would come on a white horse in a glory cloud. Then watch for the Father moves in splendor and beauty, so it will be.

You have heard Me, here I am, I come to do My Father's work. O God, that what is written of Me, make perfect everything good that is whole in Me. We will accomplish the covenant of everlasting peace. And if you failed to hear, now I said it in your ears to hear, and I will, by the Holy Spirit, open the eyes of babes to see as heavenly bodies roam in God's domain and as I come in 'eisphero klema'.

Consecrate my first supper with My new fruit grown by the light of the Morning Star. Consecrate My first supper with My new fruit grown ripe by the agelessness of God. Consecrate God by taking it to the supper and sharing its power to live in the new earth and the new heaven. What is consecrated, is illuminated by your Father, who gave Me birth in both domains; so will you who take of His things in the brilliance of light in Me, receive the light of the Morning Star. For I am all these things in Him. I prayed before the temple, the light of My Morning Star in you, perfecting in you His will. That night standing in the Garden with my own reverent fear, in the land between two pillars did I receive My answer? Among my brothers, came Satan, and all vile things hid in the shadows calling out to Me that I would never come again. And yet, I am this day through to you. But still in unbelief you push away the Word and even go into my church to be seen and heard, for your social bath. I have always known of your nakedness, and to cover it still, without acceptance is by way of sin, living in shadows.

I testify My first supper will be like the Spirit of breath upon the water, and all my teachings of the Father refreshing and restored upon the alter. This is so that you will gain lift to His holy ground. Evil will surely step away to be killed. At the sounding of Him upon His creation, Our music will burst through to your birthright. So consecrate My first supper as I did My last, with the wine being blood and the bread being My body, so that in remembrance of Me, you remain free of sin. Consecrate My supper with the Last Supper in remembrance of your first brothers and sisters who put forth for you, the Father God. Consecrate the Father God with all My blessings and all My love; as you love Me, so love Him, your true God.

The food is out of His Garden, your Father God's. For what comes out of the Garden will bring in your midst such kindness and things of seas and lands never witnessed, since the time that Adam and Eve were sent out of the Garden. I verily say, of such grace you will witness God's mighty river flowing through you, and sweeping by. In its reserve, deep pools, and swirling eddies, the backwash of jewels from heaven will be abundant for the true hand who reaches in the baptism of the 'rain bread' and of the Holy Spirit. Be raised up, as I have done, in His eternal everlasting Glory. For this is of the Father, to have His will for you, given. I will be there with all others amidst your receivership and standing amidst His will and yours. My crown was of thorns, but your crown will be of those jewels from out of the 'rain bread' that come as a river of glory.

What was fought for you was won. This you know. What is in the Spirit is real and awaits your constitution of faith and belief. Start with one hand, as I have done, and raise it up, as I did when I raised Lazarus. Raise on high the jewels you have discovered and offer them to God in heaven. I will take your jewel and place it near His throne. He will give you in return, a white stone and reveal only to you it's meaning. Share the 'rain bread', so that all can overcome in the last days, and be walking toward high-gated places of His magnificent beauty. I say this, but it could be anyone, and therefore so you know Me that I am, I will write as if you were there amongst us who first believed in the new covenant.

The ground made pure now purified, sacred now sanctified, My sacrifice given for the remission of your sin, but in freedom… lost to disbelief. You who believe are His splendor and testimonial to His betrayer, and in all creatures of God, heaven is beautified by souls who come with the bloom of faith upon them. Be baptized again in the Spirit and eat of the hidden manna!

Why would I come to an unwilling and hard heart cast in the inferno? To show you the power you have to effect their cause. I tell you the truth; I can show all hearts in belief that of a stubborn heart is easily won. I have many good and wonderful servants that I serve. This servant had one thing and only one thing I could work with; he does what he is told.

If all he does is what I tell him to do, and I am of the Father, living in the Father, then he is in grace. I have prophets, but of service to reluctance, I am close in with family and friends who prod him to do. Three of them are prophets of the Word of God. I do this to show even those who hear who will not do, can be made to by those who can. If reluctance gives way to love, what power over the defeated do you have?

This servant whom I speak of, I put into his hands the Word of God. He believes in Me, and with open-heart, loves and obeys. It is not the devotion I am honored with; it is that from disbelief he came to Me, not by reason, but by absolute doubt, but not doubt of Me, not doubt in Me, but doubt in and of himself. So finally, as he turned toward Me, he could hear and see.

I could not walk by him knowing such ignorance could easily be removed. So it is with you who know of those who have a stubborn heart for belief. You will be given more power than I, to push back ignorance, even if carnal men as intelligent, honor their disbelief. Let them have cause to doubt, as Peter doubted even as the rooster crowed.

So you will understand and know Me now, as I am, as I am then and now, look within your heart at My image and I am those good things in you. Still you who can't hear, but know Me by what is said that is given new meaning, I will tell you a parable.

The farmer did everything to grow his garden. He planted all kinds of variety of plants to cultivate a great harvest. He worked each day and into the night in the season, watching over every aspect of his farm. He worked still longer hours up to the time of the harvest. As he looked over the plentiful fruit in his valley, he knew he must have received a blessing, so he went to the river to be baptized, the first time in his life. A young pastor gladly received him into the river, and baptized him with water, and anointed him with the Holy Spirit. He was so filled with joy that he invited everyone at the baptisms to share in His crops. "Come! My crops are full and plentiful. They are tall and full of figs. At least take your share and seed for the next planting season. I expect nothing in return." The other side of the river was in drought and had no crops. This surely was a blessing to these people for they faced certain famine And so they were overcome by joy and went up with him to his land. When they arrived the locust had consumed the valley of fruit and plant. Some in their great expectation, accused him of falsehood. Others spat on the soil by which he labored, and then they turned their backs on him and said he did not receive the Holy Spirit by water or by Christ Jesus. Yet I tell you, I received him that day. A young girl ran ahead scattering the locust and pulling up the roots of each plant. She labored intensely, and others not knowing, joined in helping her gather each root until all roots were pulled up. She ordered water to be brought from the river. She fired up each vessel and they ate of the root, so that a great feast took place. After the feast, they fell asleep on the land of great abundance. Some of the root had properties to make them peace. Verily I say, when they awoke they were in My Garden.

So it is, as it has been told. Those of you who labor in the Word, and share My 'rain bread' will break all curses, and gain ground in the promised land, and be lifted holy to My holy ground, and waken in My Garden. For it is the Father's will, that this be so. Believe Me, there is not a curse that cannot be broken. Have those so afflicted pray with you in My name, and dwell in My place of restitution, and they will be made free in the wholeness of God.

Then consecrate the root of My vine and labor the vine watching over it, as it grows fruit. I give everlasting continence of the Father, so that your life can appear both in Heaven and on the earth. I give you, who take of the Word of God, an increase of His 'rain bread' and Holy Spirit with the sweat of my brow and the tears of my eyes. You will gain in freedom at light speed, washed of all sin. I will give of the Father for your submission in glory, a love so great that you will be consecrated and held on high with love always. I will give to you, who keep it protected, those things hallowed in grace and magnify your family, even in Heaven. I will give by His score your God, a word to sing, "Ja hahilai Yoshua Hosei Rheo". Let it be sung and born again unto you whom will be of My Father's new birth of heaven and earth. I give to your birth by such consecrated works, all creation. You, who labor and believe and now share from out of the Garden, will receive in Him, His complete wisdom. This will be like love blooming at light speed.

Can you look at your advancements in awe and not still understand it is I, God's covenant with you, that creates all good things out of His heart? For it is of such wisdom gifted to man, by which you survive the sin of this world. But by your decadence linked to the serpent in the Garden, you cover over the pollution and unhealthy beliefs of your world. All the riches of this world will succumb to judgment, and all wealth, as you understand it to be love, will be lifted up to My Father's throne. Yet, some of you will throw your mammon toward the heavens and attempt to buy your way in. You heard Me proclaim, "you cannot serve both mammon and God."

I cannot take what is not mine to take. I come that day to lift up the remnant of love. Be in love in God always.

I am your friend. Did you ever see the sky change colors so discretely that it had no color? It will change many times before judgment. But when judgment is done, red will be red, and green will be green, but all will be held in the white light of My Father. When you come through Me, you come before the Father, your God and your Father. What is bonded is adjoined to Him, and from out of this union and heart are all the issues of life and creation. The spectrum of no color is God's holy name, and love for you.

When one of you becomes all of you, then you will understand the way God moves. For now, He moves by His will, in an instant or all at once. So it is by His will, I come. Stand guard and be a good steward. There will be those who steer you away and tell you I am a lie. So the fruit that is picked off the vine is made into wine. But the vine produces new fruit. It is the new fruit that comes with the sweetness of glory to bring One Church before Us, and it is the old fruit made into new wine that you drink in remembrance of My work in them.

I did not come so you would not know Me. I came so you would know who I am. I gave up nothing for you, I sacrificed everything for you, you could have, in heaven, the Father's domain. I am the full measure of My Father. I am Jesus, raised first born from the dead, and I am Jesus, the Father's Glory. I fulfilled His Word. I died pure of heart with no sin. My life was not taken, but delivered unto Him who is the life. I am the life.

I broke evil's hold and false promise. I paid the price for Adam and Eve, and I freed you of sin. I gained heaven for eternity and it is yours for the taking up of the new covenant with Us. I gave up nothing and gained everything. Even you, if you come, so will I.

I went to Satan, by the Father, to gain back the Father's first right to man, a Garden full of life. I won the land, a perfect Garden in harmony with all things of God. A place where each man and each woman born to each a child, lives with the beauty of Spirit passing through like a river of plenty. Such is real gold and richness. This is what I know and only to those who have faith, will I come with the Garden. Wholeness of life is the one vine of My Father, and if you are fruit that doesn't know where it came from, then you will perish with no one knowing your sweetness.

Now, I will give you even more. God moves, from one place He can be, and to the next, so He is. To move with God, move with His will, and the flow of His Word. Still yet, I will give you more. The day I come, turn and face the beast and shout My name. Rejoice and stay in joy the day I come. If you don't believe, believe and do as I say. For all your unjust, you shout My Name at the beast in belief, and you will make it to paradise. But be as stone and be shattered that day, if you don't know that I have come. For more will be dust than foundation.

A woman was walking along looking for Me. I stopped her and asked her, "What are you looking for?" She said for her lord. I said to her, "Look no more, for I am." What you don't know was I was alive in this woman. What she saw out of her Father's heart was Me. What she heard in her heart from Me, was the Father. Now, do you believe the Father when He seeks you…for she is amongst you again? She is wise and in joy, go to her, for Zao and Zeo and the wife of Zao, who I name Rheo are prophets in Us, who are all complete, so will they be made complete by the sharing of My Words and the refreshing 'rain bread'. So you will know it true and know I have sent them, I will make attendant of My servant for this time. You will know the servant of the Lord and you will know I am such truth.

I will wed thee upon the land and in the sea, and the whole expanse of heaven. For I am Jesus, your Father, and of His Son your intercessor, and have the Spirit made holy, as hallowed is

His name. In one does Trinity reign, and by no number, not even three can you divide Us. You who can, will. And you who divide this to meaning know this: you cannot divide up God even though you think you can. God is not divisible by any number. Yet you divide the church, you divide His voice, you divide by books, and it is evil that makes you think God is more than one. When you can stop bringing God down into numbers and things, to the things of His Spirit and things of His Wisdom, then you will hold a cup full of wine from one vine. Still you divide up your body, and what body can live without a heart. So that you will know who I am, when you pray next time to Me, I will rain and wash one hundred people for you in your name. Don't tell anyone of this and believe it in your heart and you will hear it is so. I love each of you and this should tell you all to My Grace and Glory and the love of your Father. Take up the wine and the bread, take up the spirit of the fruit, take up the armor given you, and take up my commandments, take up my gifts and promises, take up my sword and raise it high above, knighting your Kingdom and your God. May this be all you need before I come. Before I come be a good steward and protect the Word with My blood.

Cover my blood over all things of God, for My Angels will appear in such places. Now come in peace.

Volume Four: Chapter One
THE GIFTS OF THE 'RAIN BREAD'

The Spirit of God has fallen on Me. I am the servant of the Lord. This is the manna of God, rained down for 40 days and 40 nights, to those who hear. I have received hidden manna and the fourth white stone. I have received it to give of it. I have received it in the light of His glory, Jesus Christ.

For it was called out to Me that the first was the resurrected Christ Jesus, the second, Paul, the third, John's receivership in Revelation. Although, those gifted are many, those saints and those honored by His name, those who are meek, those with honor who spread the good news and believe in Christ Jesus as their Savior and are in His eyes made holy by His body, now remain the brightest shade of His lamp. And I am only a witness, made over by obeying His Word to deliver, as only a messenger, His gifted anointing for the Glorious Church, as a friend, I give what has been given to Me. Now therefore, what I have received in the name of Jesus, I have received in the Holy Spirit, and I have received in the breath of the Father, such that has been ordained by His birthright to give from His lamp, His light upon you...His Church.

I stand alone, on this day, with no ambition or ego or reason, but to fulfill as He has commanded of Me. I am His servant nothing more. But see, as you seek Him and His Spirit within His lamp, and hear, and make sense of the good news. He has named this day Zao, Rheo, Zeo and I, His servant. I only add, not as the reflection of ego, but reflection of honor, that I know Him and it is my privilege to serve, for I have received and I cannot deny truth.

The Lord Jesus said, "So large is the moment, that hinges Our universe from within heaven, that both will rotate and both universe of heaven and earth by being of time, will in God's time, center itself throughout infinity, as both draw upon the center of this world toward My Coming. God will command those things witnessed by John to come to pass as an unfolding of His moment. I set out the seals to be appropriated by the Father, and I am Jesus. They will be closer to earth than heaven. But they will not open until the Father consecrates them with glory and with My blood that is held in store for this time. When opened so it will be by the sound of His angel, that I send two of My angels to do His work in preparation of My coming".

I am the servant of the Lord and this is what I heard, as put forth, by Him… the Glory of Peace. "It will be like no other sign. For I am the sign and I am Jesus. You who share the good news, now share the good news made over by your Father: that health by the Word of God will overcome, and no obstacle will be left to you, but all will be faith. My dove will be two angels and I will send them ahead. The Angels will do the work of God where oceans will be restored, and the land will run like a river, and the life will scatter and be made whole in His breath. Yet none of you, but those who receive a white stone, will know its full meaning. As by him, who obeys and prays that you will know, so it is I, working through My prophets, that the message of this white stone is received and understood. Yet, because he who obeys did not consummate the meaning in his heart, he will forever need the Holy Spirit to lead him, and those in My spirit to interpret those things that come to him. But you who can take now his prayer fulfilled, as each My messenger's, can receive understanding, and if you are asked, then share My Word with My servant. In this, the white stone is made complete in the presence of My body."

I have prepared him to listen, and he has given of his heart to Me, so I cannot ignore My servant's need to hear and deliver My command. Now understand this, those of you who are Israel made over by the 'rain bread', what is revealed is to fulfill the promise of God, your Father, and My harmony. His grace is His mercy as I am born of His mercy; I am born again within His wrath to judge sin. So it is now, as I said it would be: the light pours as rain upon My body, washing the remnant, and preparing the day. Let this white stone carry clearness of His holy waters.

My mother was Mary, and I was neither the seed of Judea, nor Rome, but I was whole of all Israel. Like you were once dust of this earth and that of heaven, I was made complete in His hallowed Name. I was made the image of God in man, born from a womb like man, but first of His heavenly womb, born in Mary by her faith. Mary believed the scriptures and honored them with the Son of man. Yet, she knew she carried the Son of God. So strong was her faith that she received the will of My Father. Let the record show that it cannot be argued, that the house of God can ever be divided; what fell out of His grace is now disgraced in the bowels of this world, but not of Our house. I was lifted from the day I was in her womb, to the day of My resurrected self. Now you know the truth.

So you will know Me, I will tell you this: by the same act as My birth, I live in your midst, and I have entered into God's covenant made over in glory, to leave my instructions to My servant. God has struck His power into the lamp and seven shades of light will come forth. One shade prevails in My witness, and another shade prevails in Zao, Rheo, and Zeo.

From small beginnings, such glory will arrive. Then there will be three others, again seeking My Star. They will seek this shade of light and take it to the land by which My remnant will gather before the Holy Glory of Israel. Then will my two angels appear and wash with glory the land and the sea of My remnant. I will be the seventh shade, and I will be formed in a cloud as I ride of My Father's horse, to do His final will. Satan will hear this, and he will read it, and yet he will never understand it, nor know His days are numbered to the end of time. Be of sin and you will go out with the end, and never know the truth of the Father's plan for a new beginning.

So you will know it is Me, I told you the meek will inherit the earth. Those seeking My Star, will be a remnant of glory. It will be the just, not the unjust, who will see My Morning Star. In the garden of Gethsemane, I saw My Star come forth with the sounding of God, and it was peace, complete of will and command, complete of everlasting love, and infinite command. So you will see, who believe in Me, such things of God.

I tell you the truth: this is like a child, who upon seeing either parent knows peace within love. Even those who are abandoned, abused, even tortured to death as babes, helpless and without the means yet to walk… so are those, by My Father's grief of such acts of sin, given over to heaven in His complete peace and restoration, knowing nothing of wrong or harm, but only knowing infinite peace. This is Our love for you. So it will be for those who suffer in My name and are persecuted because of Me. But you who take of My good name, and benefit this day… have your heaven. So give of it, and all will go well for you. Take and never give, and nothing will be given to you of heaven.

One day, there will be a cloud of My Father and with it My army. Justice will be served upon all wrong doings and sin scorched to nothing. My Morning Star is made over in heaven as in Us, a simple garden for My remnant. Be of that remnant when I come.

Now, so you will know it is Me who commands My seven gifts unfolding, look to My glory for the rain to wash in, and take these Words as the white stone shared upon My mantle, prayed for and now delivered upon by a simple witness. How then is it, that such can be done, even with so little faith? I tell you the truth: this servant was not born as I was, but served without knowing, as many do, the fallen one. By his testimony, he walks in My name today, God is now master of his soul, and will keep him a shade of light, so you will know it is Me, the first born from the dead. My name is Jesus upon the land of all Israel.

The days of glory are upon you! Do not deny what is given, for you will prolong what is to be only by bringing misery to your need. Untold sin will spread like locust that blinds a false sky. For clearly the sky of My Father never changes His glory or light, but His sky can, like His light, be withdrawn. The four corners of the earth will be given the 'rain bread' in defense of such wickedness to come. It will purge all sin, but it will do nothing if it is not received. The Word of God will prevail, however, and the 'rain bread' will remain a gift against the locust. It is your will, now to do as God's will, and it is in Us, to obey and give the full measure of the 'rain bread'.

So now you will forever remain knowing it is I who consecrated these gifts by My Father's grace, the 'rain bread' has poured out on heaven upon you. I will give to its call and to its nature the forty parables of the nations, which arise to the one place of the Father, all Israel. It is the work I did after I left John the Baptist for this very time, and it has come, and so be it, I will come in God's time. So it will be the same for Me, My Morning Star, and My Father, and His Spirit. Amen.

Volume Four: Chapter Two: APECHO

Know My teachings by the Word of God.

I am alive. I am in your midst. From now until the end of time, the heavens shine brightly at my return. I have been raised in glory by the Word of My Father, and this day I pour out fulfillment of the 'Rain Bread' for you to receive. Call out My tribute to those who carry within them the Holy Ghost, and to those who believed in Me, but were slain by evil and are now risen to Us by Him who created all heaven and earth. They join My heavenly host, those who were father's and mother's before you. For they are risen, to bring forth the fruit in the Garden, to Our newcomer's. It is a glorious day in heaven. They are first of those in rest. This is your day of glory on earth as it is in heaven, and those prayers, now served on those gone at the hand of Satan, are this day restored. By your Father, come forth, be made whole, unto heaven. As you press into the Glory, you will see and hear even more than this… be walking in God's love.

But for you on earth, it is the last chance to be washed in the spirit of His Word. Come clean My children. Take up your need of the Garden and your need for hospitality and your need to know God. Your need is filled to the brim this day, and it will runneth over by the end of day. See as the setting sun, I will rise over this world.

John put before you My path, and that of the Father, and the Holy Ghost. A woodsman cut a path through the woods, but he cut one path true and the one path false. John, however, cut only one path true. The woodsman after a few days took off to admire his clever scheme to trick his neighbor. He forgot how good his deceit and walked the false path off the cliff. You cannot walk falsely on the path that was shown to John, for I laid down for you, the direction to Me.

The things of the sea are not of the land, yet the remnant is both. You are of God and not of Satan, but it is by sin that you are Satan's and it is by God that you are a God child. How is it that Satan has so many of you by your own will, when it is the will of God that you have your will in life, not death?

A tree that yields no fruit will perish without a name. When you go to the well to draw wate,r you will be filled by the measure of your thirst and your hunger. Know this to be true: Satan did not overcome Me by thirst or by hunger...for when he tempted Me by thirst it was My hunger for God that won over him, and when he tempted Me by hunger, it was my thirst of God that won over him. So it is, with you who, overcome.

Come walk with Me...I am walking in God's Garden, and I am fulfilled. So can you be...Here! I receive your prayers and act accordingly to each measure by God's command. It is I, who take your prayers before God, and it is God, who sends Me to answer prayers. So you shall know it is Me, I will teach you of things God created to restore His glory, and to regain His children. These are things that only I know, and those things now in motion, given to My body, you will know.

I name John the Baptist to proclaim it and send upon this earth new bread, made from the old bread, now refreshed. Hear him for it is My Word. For John is in the good book, now made alive before you, as all the fathers, and all the mothers before you, are now refreshed and alive. Go to the good news and see how much they are in glory. For each are the children of God, and each are His legacy to win back you to His Garden.

I knew a woman who lost her husband and her farm all at the same time, within days of each other. She went into town and offered herself to the first man she found. The man was a hard worker. He told her to come back on the Sabbath. She had to labor to wait, for it was still only the first day. When the day finally arrived, she showed herself and the man took her in, not for lust, but as a wife because she waited for him.

Now, I tell you this: so you can know the other side. I knew a man who took another woman as a wife for lust, and she took him for all the gold he had. Neither the man, nor the woman lived as the other, for a man is a man and a woman is a woman, so by thirst and hunger they perished dying the same death. I tell you the truth: when you sin, you are consummated to death and wedded to evil. You never live your life in marriage under evil. You cannot live in adultery and be born again to Me. Stand right before God and ask for His forgiveness. Serve your divorce, or wed again, but don't play your affairs as trickery or you will perish on the day of judgment. It is better for you to be a woman in life, and a man in life, than a man of sin or a woman of sin. It is better for you to be yourself in Me.

Listen more, and learn My manna. As I teach, I know a woman who labors over her work and a man who labors over his work. It is by God that they have been given these gifts. Both can endure much. They spend all their time making ready their wares to sell in the marketplace. They are diligent, and by endurance they succeed. But I tell you, if they were to spend one second out of one hour in the Word of God seeking My Father, their market goods would sell 10-fold. For the love of labor and good works does not replace, either by faith or by word, the love of the Father. You must love My Father to know who I am, and I am the labor of His love.

It will go well in these times for you who seek God with all your heart, mind, and soul. Everything hinges on manifesting God's love on earth. Come forth, take of it, and give of it. The earth is in His midst of heaven, and I will come in glory to the earth.

My outpouring of the 'rain bread' is upon you, so that you may claim it. Shout it! Take of it! Let it be shared through and through until the glory of it is manifested in Me, My Father's Spirit, in all heavenly creatures of My body. Now so that you will understand what I am telling you I have a parable to share. Take of it both Meanings:

There was a king who desired blessing and a abundance for his people. He knew his people were bonded to the wrong things, however, so his kingdom was not free, even though his people moved from here to there without restraint. Yet, they accepted paying taxation. They paid to the unjust. They indulged the unjust. They catered to the unjust. The king's people didn't know him or his thoughts. Yet many who lived before him told the people repeatedly that the king would come and lay down his life for them. And so he did.

You know, that one day the king walked out of his palace and the people gathered around to see if he would bless them with more of his wealth. But he brought the wealth of heaven, and he spoke in the authority of His God, the God of Abraham, and they did not know the newness of his words. He spoke the word over his kingdom. Still, his voice rang only as loud as they tolerated, waiting for his offerings and gifts. But nothing moved them to the next glory.

So they brought their sick people to him, their children, and their sadness. Because they thought he could not give them all they wanted, they turned their back on him. They walked away from their king. The king returned to his palace alone. Not one citizen came with him on his journey home. And one day the king looked over his city and he wept. He had seen the stone to his palace fall. He thought he would die of a broken heart when his God spoke, "I am your friend and you have arrived into your kingdom of all Israel, and it is magnificent in every corner of its unlimited domain. This is your kingdom, and your people will come by the millions as My Word restores the palace walls. Just after the river overflows it's banks, you will see that you have won. Now rest and take heart, as the unfolding of My will charges those who are death, and those who bow to Your name. You will flow to them in My 'rain bread' and each will wash in My Word."

There is the meaning of the Word and there is the meaning of God's purpose. How is it that you who exalt Me on high? Yet you don't understand when it comes to your life, that My Father needs to exalt you to His kingdom, because like Me, your Father loves you. You will be charged in the days of glory, but not condemned or judged. You are given your charge, and it is either yes or no, nothing in between can pass through to heaven. Either you are born again seeking My council in those things God puts before you, or you are dead where you walk. It has never been any different. God seeks a relationship with each of you. Seek His truth and for that, be saved by His truth.

You might be of a mind where you judge the giver of such parables as simpleminded, possibly a false prophet, an imposter, or worse…a puppet working for Beelzebub. I tell you the truth: many have written as I have ascribed them to, and every inspired writer has been tested by time and has done My Father's will as even I directed it to be done. Now you know the truth. If you are in God's will you have the power of God to move upon a mustard seed of faith and push Satan back into the sea. As even mighty Rome found out, faith moves mountains.

Be careful not to judge another. I say if you judge another you have judged yourself. For you are only as strong as the weakest amongst you. So bear up those weak to be stronger than yourself, and you will rise mighty before the throne of God. So then, David grew his glory from such understanding…

I knew a man who went to great length to make the best bread in all the land. The oven temperature had to be just so. The oven itself had a special dome-construction, and the moisture had to be just so, and the dough filled with the best flour, and the yeast was new. The news traveled quickly that he had the best bread. People came from all over to have a broken-off piece. But there was a boy who put his bread on a rock and it raised with no effort, even higher than the famous bread of the day. The man heard of this and came by, and scoffed at the boy's bread, and publicly denounced it. He claim it would not be full or merit much taste. I took of the boy's bread and was instantly fulfilled.

Raise up not from false heights.

Some ask if I show up at burials, to look on at funerals, to be there for them. This is the work of My angels. I have never buried a life or attended death. Let the dead bury the dead, for I am the everlasting life, and I receive life. So it is, only those in whom I celebrate life, that I attend. Now live, for I am the life.

Once a man claim an infestation of rats took away his family, and he wept on the streets for his wife and child. But as the rats closed even upon him as he wept, he chose to utter My name, Jesus, and I raised him to his wife and child. This is done when the will of the Father moves time itself, before death strikes. So it is, when the wicked come to steal away life, and life is struggling before death, that I will come with the gift of life and restore even in the moment of forgiveness, those gripped by evil, who can claim My name; they will claim paradise.

Weddings are a time to celebrate, but your wicked generation makes many a funeral. For I knew two people who wedded under My name, but their purpose was whatever they wanted My name to be. So like the new wine skin with new wine, they filled as they drank. By the hour, My name became les, and so it was true of their marriage. By morning, the rooster that would crow was found hung and those wedded under false pretense were not awakened to life. I will attend fewer weddings like these.

You might conclude that I am hard on rock, and this would be truth. Yet, even as I speak to outcome, I must share with you a story…

There were two neighbors who had the power of governance in their town. They governed a complete doctrine of righteousness. Their town received a constant seamless flow of water, blessings, and gifts, but not because of their governance, but because a few received God into their hearts. I tell you the truth… a seed is planted, then receiving water, the seed planted grows mostly when it receives the light of day. The river of God's Word grows the valley of Eden in your midst. Shout down the Garden of Eden. Claim it! Make it yours and make of it by your own labor to plant back the seed, and restore the land with the vine, and make of the sea pure and clean. Uncover the soil and let it breathe God in. Plant and sow, and water, and wash in My Word, and receive My light for growth.

Still, the bold and the brave soon pick up and leave, even as they lived around Me and attended My work. After awhile they begin to believe it is them that lead the way. A man is pleased with what he can create, but it was God who gave him the gift. Yet he takes all the credit, and he polishes and adores his creation. He cherishes not even his talent, but more his work of art. By the time his life is over, what was stored up in heaven for him, even more beautiful than his work of art, is given to the man who worshipped God first before all things. That man will receive double his offering, and the man who loved his art work will get nothing more.

Nothing false will get into heaven. Only truth aligned to God will arrive at the gate. And even with that, only a handful will pass through the gate in truth, if the sins of this world are not washed in the Word of God. So be alert, and beware, for many more can enter into heaven than even now, if they worship the God of Abraham. For this is the God who created you.

You might like to know, even I, like good music. And why not? For God designs and makes music, as so does His choir. A woman took Me by My hand and led Me to a group of performers. She commented on how sweet the music was and how well the stage was set, and how much life came from the performers. I agreed with her. Each player was of value and each gifted. The music made for excitement and dance. I followed her into the music and the dance. I danced before God in my heart, and enjoyed the day as it retreated into night. Even I find joy in such things. Bring God to your feast, dance, and music, for God loves the merriment of His people; for the day He attends, I will attend... for the day He comes, I will come.

This I will do for you, take My hand. Let yourself drift. We are together. I take you to the edge of My land and we sit down. I pick up a seashell and blow into it. I tell you this: the waves of the sea are like the music of heaven; and so is the music of God's rain, both the sounding of His Spirit and the silence of His name. A great peace stirs your God, when in your ear, He sounds. Now, you know how to hear the Word.

This I will do for you... I weep. I wept to cleanse myself. And I was washed by the tears of My Father the day I entered into heaven. God weeps, as I weep. Amongst you is sweetness and beauty, but the noise is greater from the gnashing of teeth. So great is the noise of life gone to us, when we weep our tears cause rivers in heaven to overflow? From the rivers of His holy waters, a torrent comes to purge and sweep My washed people up into God. For each who believe in Me are My body and in My body contains the land of people dear and nearest to Me. So when My body is washed up to God, so then will you be.

You ask questions that keep you from your life. I will answer you, so you can move on… for I call you now to spread the good news refreshed by My Spirit. You ask Me what will the battle be like? I tell you the truth, for no one will escape My battle. A powerful ruler sat upon a throne and he ruled with an iron fist. All was accounted for. All was measured. All was put to work for more gain upon gain. All marched to the ruler's command. All took orders with pride. All executed those orders without fear. All took life. All were loyal. All were hailed brave and had beautiful wives and children. All were rich with trappings. All were of the rulers higher order. All met with My wrath. All were found in the instance of My coming. All were judged according to their ruler's sin. The ruler of sin fell to the light of judgment. Yet, it is a bigger battle for you to seek Me and have a relationship with the Father, than the contest of My battle. For evil is so great and entwined with the days of glory, that now even the apple is a brilliant red, instead of the just fruit of God.

Take heart in the Word of God, and you will draw unto Us, and We will draw closer to you, even as you battle the wicked world and the false order.

Know this to be true: the world is composed of many beautiful places; places, even now, remain near to the Garden. Even a remnant of the Garden is here on earth. Nations upon nations within their boundaries have, even now, as I speak, a path to the Garden. Know beauty and gain knowledge of the Word of God. Know thy Father and thy Mother. It is My Church born of Me, that thy Mother is to thy Father. For she held Me in Her womb, and I came unto you, in the flesh, now I come unto you as the everlasting light of My Father from out of My church. He has given Me birth through His Holy Spirit. I am complete in all things of His.

Know where you are and where you are going. You cannot live in two places at once. You can only live in the midst of My Father to truly live one moment of heaven and earth.

So you will understand, nation upon nation, and church upon church, and even each of you who are uniquely different come to the likeness of My Father. Bring your assemblies under one roof, bring even those to the rooftop that can come through the roof. For My house will take all.

There was a farmer who went to sleep at night and when he awoke the locust struck. He could do nothing to save his field of crops. He was bankrupt in the moment of the Morning Star. For he hung on his door two gnarly things of Satan. I come to right the unjust things, even things of possession. Even those things you look at are recorded. I tell you, you might know someone who counts the very fraction of the world that they themselves take ownership of and horde it for themselves. Don't let them count you as theirs. You are God's child and free to give and receive all things of the Father's.

Any of you and all of you can take up as teachers, pastors, evangelists, apostles, prophets, and servants. Any of you and all of you can have heart and mind in worshipping My Father. My Father is your Father. All of you have a share in His Word. Sit if you need to be filled and stand if you need to be heard, but don't sit or stand for want of ambition over another. For I have seen you become territorial, even over sitting arrangements, taking priority over others to get near your pastor. All of you are in the Word and the Word of God is shared equally. All of you can have all your Father has to give, none more than some.

You might understand this by My work and by those things foretold. I come to those even in your prisons. If they will ask forgiveness, and in repenting call My name in belief, I come instantly and fill the heart. For I am Jesus, and anyone who calls My name to be saved, is saved. You might know someone who counts the very fraction of the world that they believe they own. I verily say unto you, they can count each grain of sand, and even count the stars if they wish, but they cannot count you as theirs, for you are a child of God. You are free to be His child.

You charge for the gifts given you to make your living. I walked by many flowers on earth perfected by My Father. But some flowers lose their blooms quickly. Others break off after a storm. Others are knocked down to the mud after a hard rain, and they lose their luster. There are many ways to stand against sin with the gifts you are given. Now go, and give of your gifts, adding onto another, for this is the giving of gifts by His image. This is the first act of the Garden. God gifted the Garden to you.

Are you so different? Can you not see the likeness in all things of God? If the difference that you so judge is so different from the place you judge, I will remove you from your high place and you will fall back into the sea and be no different than the sea. For the body of My Church is one body, not two.

Your thirst reminds Me of a man I came to know on my way to Damascus. He cried that the well was dry. I told him to get his own water. He cried that the well was dry. I told him to drink of the sand. None of this is known or understood. He sank and looked bewildered. I asked him, "why do you persecute Me?"

He cried out from his heart. I struck him with My charge and he obeyed. His heart was made to flow with water. For I am the source and from My heart flows all of salvation. Even as Satan claims you by a name, I rename you by God. So I give you three names, Zao, Zeo, and Rheo. Now you know who will first prophesy the 'rain bread'. Each to take of it, will receive their name in Me. For My name is above all others.

I knew a woman who guarded a storehouse. She had stored all her worldly possessions in the house. Every day she would unlock her storehouse and count all she had. When she died she could neither take it to heaven, nor to the grave. But you can take the Word of God to heaven.

I tell you these things so you can truly understand; this is the hour of glory and I have poured out My 'rain bread' for you to prepare cleansing of My Church. So what is in a day is not in a life, yet you toil in the day fearing the worry that will kill you. I tell you the moment you live is life, and you can have a relationship with God and have a spirited life. I have seen people who toil in the sun near death hoping for their crop to come in, but even a seed will stay dormant without water. The water I speak is the Word of God.

You have been given life. Isn't life the most exalted treasure of being that God can give? If you were given all Israel, all heaven, and all the vast riches of God, and all the rain of God, would you pick this for yourself knowing that you chose over a life with God?

Not one, no not one of you, would trade such riches for life. It is by His life with God that you exist at all, and it is by His Grace that you receive such gifts.

So it is in My coming that I am received, and you will see the bright Morning Star. I will compare this to a butterfly. Most of you are amused at seeing the butterfly in flight. Neither do you know its purpose nor its meaning, but you name the thing by a word. I verily say by His Word you are so named, but you are more than flight. Believe Me when I say this, for your name is beauty and its truth is a life in God. The lift of His Spirit adorns your wings .By His light you are made His hallowed name. Some of you see the light of heaven, and some of you hear the rain pour, and some of you both see and hear and know His glory is pouring out into the earth. I say to anyone of you… now see and hear! Look at the light bouncing in the clouds and sky above, it is your sunlight, made by the same light of heaven. From His light you were created. So how is it that you cannot see or hear, when by His Word you are made whole in His glory and in His beauty.

Here I am. I am the good and just, who's light is brilliant and radiates through and through, holding all things of God's creation together. I will give you in the Word of My Father, hidden manna, and it will shine My light of glory upon the good news so that you will understand. It has always been there from the beginning, but even as you polish a rock, so does glory shine to the next moment a more radiant path to truth. There is no new doctrine in that I am constant, and have been so from the beginning.

I walked with a woman who could neither make up her mind to know the errors of her way, let alone to know the way of My Morning Star. Confusion will blind you from seeing or hearing. This woman was without direction, neither did she know the path she was on or the one she left. I asked her even her name and she knew it not. You cannot call to one without a name. So I named her, and by a simple name she became filled with living water and lives a good life. I tell you: if you care to name one in My name to those things of My Father, you will reap a reward of such beauty for yourself that by such beauty you become filled with glory light. And those around you will honor you and know you to be made wealthy in My name.

By such light you will move life, even your own, to a place above the world. In such a place you will be given a body that knows no limits. But, even today, your body knows no limits… even now, even as you age, for you don't know it is the dust created by the light of the Father, and by such dust you are worthy of such light, and by faith, the light restores even your age to eternal youth. I give this to you now… old, and young alike.

What is in a day is not in a life, yet you toil in the day with fear and worry over those things that will kill you. Take up with Me and live your spirited life with God. I tell you the truth: you can be named Muhammad and know the God of Abraham. It is all about the Father…but if you worship Muhammad, and not the Father, then you do not know the Father. Verily I say unto you, I will raise from rest Muhammad, and wash, and oil his feet…as I will for each of you, who has a relationship with My Father. I know this as I know all time, Muhammad bows before Me and washes both my feet and oils them with his joy. For I know of such things through the Father. So you know the power of My prophecy. From rest, by his sight, behold… he knows Me and he will come before the throne of My Father claiming Me to God. You are not wrong to seek the Father by way of Muhammad, for he identifies Him. Seek God first, and then you will know it is as I am. But it is by My Spirit that gifts your Father's spirit.

I tell you the truth: all Islam will join Muhammad through the gates of heaven who come by My name and take up My faith. There will be many who do, and they shall receive passage into the Garden. I will tell you beyond the Garden there is a city, that like a many-faceted diamond, with color, and with light, there are rooms for everyone. Also your body is made youth, and your day is forever.

There is no division in heaven and their should be no division on earth, for you now have been told. I am Jesus, and it is I who have spoke these words beyond the grave, from heaven, and into my servant.

Ask yourself... did God command of you to love only him with all your heart, soul, and mind? And if you did this, having a relationship with Him, honor the command. God did not forsake man or woman in His time; men who lived before Moses, sought God. Men who were born near the Garden, but didn't know His Garden, tilled their own garden and gave thanks. Neither should you condemn a man who has no faith, nor a man who has a different faith. For it is the relationship with God that God will honor. But know this: it is through Me, Jesus that you are received in My Father's house. It is the will of your Father, and I obey it, as I am. I am with God... His Son Jesus. You are My brothers and sisters. Now know Me as I am. I am the life, inside and outside. Those who seek Me, seek My Father. And I am within the hearts of those believing, pouring out the 'rain bread' so you could be glorified, and walk in the kingdom of heaven. God has given unto Me the resurrected power of life, and the judgment of death. I come for life.

Still those of you who choose to toil in the sun nearer to death, hoping your crop comes in, will toil ever closer to its furnace. For you worship only what you want, and not the water that fills your need. Even a seed will stay dormant without water. Now I will tell you what you can do to live a blessed life: water with the Word of God and live spirited with much fruit, by which you have more than enough to give and to share.

I can tell you, Muhammad was a bright and honorable man, who by his own means sought the Father and strayed from Me. He did not know who I was, but by My Father's grace, he will know who I am, and I am the life.

Know this, I have not lost even the sheep that stray. I am, and all I am is given in My deliverance of those who took My Father's Word into this earth. Everyone is accounted for. Those of you who stray with God in your heart will come up to Me. Upon seeing that I am, you will be saved if you believe. I cannot help you if you turn away from Me, for I am the life.

I tell you the truth: as I am the keeper of time, I will not lose one of my people who understand it is I. Even at rest, I will raise them by My side, so they will know that it is I. I am Jesus. Even brothers and sisters will be among you to bring you out of rest. For the meek shall inherit the earth, remember as I told you so. And the last will be the first of you to be raised to My Father's heaven. But I say unto you: I have raised those where your Father found mercy upon, and they have come before His throne, and reside in His Garden.

Know this; it is I who bless all nations into Israel. I watch for Islam, and all nations who seek the Lamb, to seek Me. For I am the Lamb. Come to the Father and you will know Me.

And those of you who seek Me on your own account, seek My Father, and I will come with your reward. I speak to you, follow the same God the Father of Abraham, Jacob and Isaac for I am He the Son of God, from whose Father of Abraham you know and all before you and after you who believe I Am. It is time to know who I am, and become not two seas, but one. I am telling the truth, for I will only return upon one sea when I come.

There will be no closure when I come. The sea of My Father will be the renewed water of heaven, but such sea that is layered beneath will remain beneath. I come to stand on a mound, and from such heights, let those to be seen by all who can see, gather, and I will be near to them. My foot will strike the rock, and beneath my feet the earth will swallow up the dirge and the evil of such dirge. No dome will cover My heaven or My earth. For all will be God's domain.

I bless you with all the gifts of My Spirit, and I share My drink. So now it is up to you, for you now are told by My heart… the one that beats the pulse of life in you, and the one who will raise My friends as a friend, will raise even you, who now turn to Me.

So you will know that it is I Am, as I will appear, the book of Daniel by its layer, is closed until God opens. The seals will await the Father to open. You yourself know, that Satan can twist the very best intention…Daniel knew Satan would twist the truth, and even in right-standing, a man would come and preach differently, claiming yet another God, even another division of My faith. Even those who twist My Word, to a new division, will not understand as I walk by them. Satan will twist the word of man, but he cannot twist the Word of God. He can twist your way, but he cannot twist My way. I am the way, and the only true path. No other teacher can teach you from beyond the grave, for none exist. I am truly alive without a grave. So you will be, who seek My truth.

I will make your way easy. For the 'rain bread' is the heavy rain, and it floods into the earth with light. New water to restore clarity and purity in My Word, now comes from a time that was written of long ago.

I ask you, how can the creator stand in the foliage of a birth that ends in death? What is unjust is never just… Even as a birth is still-born, I am a silent witness from the beginning. I have given birth to life, and to life, a free will. I witness, as you have, the unjust suffering. I weep still. Until the day I come, you go in wisdom to witness against those things unjust. You will attest to… the day I come… those unjust things of evil, and I will right unjust suffering and death, and rewrite justice. For justice I am. Even as I walked amongst you, I gave the wisdom to live a just life. Now, you have the wisdom to live an everlasting life. Now it is I who walk again for you, even this hour and this day forward, I walk for you. You must press forward toward such a life to understand you have no limits, and now as you live, you have even as I am, all that I am. You do many things in My name. Some of those things are your own creation and some the invention of Satan. Those of you who name Me like the butterfly, name Me Ra, Allah, Yahweh, El Shaddai, Elohim, and El, even more… now seek Me to perfect your hearing. I am Jesus, the Father and the Spirit made complete. I said, "question Ra as God." Go and seek the land of Israel. What did you expect to find? I have always been your God. As I told you as it is written when you see Me you see the Father for I am in the Father and the Father is in me…

For you I created above all else, a place for your spiritual freedom, so your own self-will could be free. I could not break a covenant that I am as I am free. So will you be. Those who remain aligned to My will, have triumph, as I did, over him, the master of trickery. You are now free of him, and yet many of you keep his company, and this is by your own choice. There is no division in heaven, so there is no division in earth. Raise up to My name, and live complete. For out of Egypt, I roamed until I could walk amongst you, and even now I walk amongst you toward the day I come, sounding from heaven against Satan. Be not on his side when I come. I will not come for peace, but to raise up my sword, and race forth with my army to arrest all evil and I will cast it into the fiery pit of hell.

Don't fear because you are Egypt, or Islam, or of another nation, who does not know who I am. When I come, I will cast the unjust and wicked into hell… fear that you are My people who still know Me not. For if you are Jewish and reside in My Land of Israel, but you do not believe in Me, woe to you… for you will see those in Egypt come, and those who are Islam come, and those who are gentiles who come, and those you judge not worthy will come on their own accord, and all who come believing Me will come to My throne. Israel is not a land closed to any person, as I am a respecter of no one, but My Father. Anyone who carries My name in their heart comes to My place of heaven. My Church will be raised into glory and His splendor, and all nations will be united on this earth, restored in My Nation, and given their reward. You who have been chosen, now have been warned: you who won't let go ill seeds, so you will be consumed by such age, but those kindred to My Spirit will be rekindled, renewed, and refreshed forever and ever. Those who have another god, will go the way of their other god. There is no other, for I am. So, they will not have a way, but an end. I am the life, and those who seek Me, seek the way to the Father. I have cleared a path for you who believe in Me.

Open up your heart, Israel! You are proof I am, but only as I choose you, now you remain blind, and I have lifted the fog that blinds you. For it is I, who comes before you to show you My church is on the move. Still, you think with doubt. Still, you fight evil with your own brand of evil. So I say woe to you, for you will live even harder times, and yet you could have life and live easily amongst your brethren. I have come this way, to reach you for the last time before My dawn. This is the "rain bread" and I will give you its parable of light within Him, who by the Word, gave light to the expanse and within the light… even My birthright, to become in Him… His light now revealed to you, that I am Jesus. I am revealed to you. Honor Me by, such honor given this simple servant, who by heart shared My fruit, bread, wine, and now cultivates its root to grow up the vine. So it is given.

Hear Me

The glory of My Father is in My blood and in My Body, and the bread is full and ready to eat, and the water to make the wine is pure. By My blood you will learn of heaven's perfection and you will never know evil's perfect sin.

The wide wing of God will grace you who believe in Me, and blind you from the horror of Satan's death, who stand in My place as I have, for the poor, the blind, the down-trodden, and the sick and lame. Go forth and get under My wing, receive My mercy. I ask you, can the harlot give her service for free?

Here is the truth: I have authority over all sin and her service is never for free, but comes with a sacrifice and a price. I paid the price in full, and I will not be compromised. When I come, it will be you who will pay who remain in sin. Those of you who take of her service for free, ignore My commands. Woe to you.

There are seven forms to heaven and one form to death, so now life and death are not hidden. The seven forms of heaven are not divided, but flow as one sea, but even a sea has a range and a depth. Death is barren, a place worse than the last, and by extreme heat, does each rung downward worsen deaths exposure to Satan.

I will tell you a story: one woman came to heaven knowing My name. One woman went to death; she fell beneath for her part in growing up Satan's harlot. I did not come to trap wealth in My name, but I came among you to give the wealth stored up in heaven for you. It is not hidden, but shines through even as the best of earth jewels can glow, the jewels of heaven radiate filled with allure and wealth. Even now you can have of them, but have of them to give away, and more will be given, that you may exchange such gifts of heaven for things of this earth. Those who hide away My treasures for the people of God, will perish without gold, or silver to dress them. I will open the vaults and pour into poverty that which is locked up in My name. You will see Me in My full dress, and I am giving of all I have.

I have already given you other places that rain diamonds, but the diamond is not the rare wealth that I uphold. One man bought his wife the largest diamond in the world, and it weighed her down. The light of this diamond faded, but I give you My light to lift you, and it is you who outshine the largest diamond in the world. Remember this always, you who have a relationship with Me, are those things made beautiful, and nothing that I have created is of such beauty as the light of My Father. For all things that I do are of the Father. All I am, is of the Father. By His heart I am life. I am the life.

One woman gave birth to Me. As I am her witness, she is in heaven now, as I tell you that Mary loved all her children. But one woman is even higher in heaven, for she gave birth to My name, witnessed My birth, put out straw for My bed, and gave My family shelter from the night. The woman who warned Herod of My birth will she find forgiveness? Say yea! But to say no and she will be gnashing her teeth until the day Satan is overcome. Make your yes be yes and your no be no when you see me. All else is of Satan.

So that you understand, there is a woman who attends and nurtures with loving kindness the foundation of My body. I will come to raise her. But woe to the woman in false labor: for she believes even in her lie, as I am truth. I was born out of the labor of man, for his sake, that he could till the soil again free of thorns. The woman labors at lies and deceit will give birth to the one against Me. He will come twisted from the day he was conceived, and his yoke broken over the wage against life, he will capture up the world in sin never yet seen. I tell you the truth: like Rome, he will perish, but not before the master of sin appears clothed in his serpent skin. I tell you the truth: if all My people, now come to Me for My name sake, gathered against him, he will perish, as all come forward without division.

Again you have a choice, but the apple he tricks you with is red by your own blood. The apple I give you, is still just an apple off the tree of knowledge, so that you can now direct your life against evil. You must pray that you will do this. Eat of your Father's fruit, before the one against Me gives you his apple of death. It looks brightly red, but how can this illusion of death lure you?

For you now have knowledge and wisdom against his coming. Know this: the plain apple on the tree of knowledge is the answer you seek to life. I will not let the serpent trick you like this again, not unless you find trickery in death a pleasure…and I know this to be not true. I made you seeking truth not death, so you would be false to think otherwise. Some of you like the serpent's skin, and I can do nothing to save you. I am the Father by heart. By your heart, now come to life. Here rain the seven shades of light in a parable to protect you from evil and give you understanding of My truth. Here is My Word of Glory: The rain pours a bounty of living light in My Word, and the Word of God glows as a jewel never before witnessed, not even so at My resurrected self. For My Word is the living light within. So you can speak of this, these parables understand the beauty within you.

In My walk, a child took Me by the hand and invited Me in to see his family. The family welcomed Me with an open heart, and they shared with Me all that they had harvested that day. I ate and drank well, and I lived good in their company. I asked them," how is it that this side of the valley had rivers, fertile soil to make wine with, and mountains to climb and be refreshed by, and lakes to bathe in, and ponds to swim in, so that everything was a washed… even the grass was a stronger blend, and the life of every living thing was of better stock…even better than the valley known for its great harvest?" First the Father spoke, "So it is, where My Spirit remains."

I asked, "How so?" Then the mother replied, "What remains alive, gives birth to His Word and creates the path of glory that you are on."

I took my own hand as the Son. I came and asked the people in the valley to till the soil and plant seeds, sowing and harvesting, and to give each in need of the harvest. My sister spoke, "I have seen the birth of this valley in the low and meek. All things first small, shine the brightest." I was amazed in the glory. My child spoke, "I see the Morning Star." When I looked up at the mountain, at first I saw three prophets of old. Through the eyes of God, I became, and as the Son, I was resurrected in God, made complete and whole of Him. Now I am the grace upon the valley floors raising to each prophet of My making, a mountain to God. This is the path I set before you. Never again will the wind blow away a thing of God. Never will you walk in a valley that is low. Each valley is raised and each mountain is made low, until all walk equally-yoked. Come forth out of brick and mortar. Come forth out of division. Come forth and gather wisdom as you come. Come forth unto the land and I will come by your side. Come forth in your belief and be made right. For if you seek God, you seek Me, and I am Jesus made over by His light to be Him. Therefore, My name is a shade of light. My Nation is a nation of My people seeking Me as their God. I am those things just and good. So how is it that My Nation can fight for freedom and still be shackled like a wild beast?

You have been given a Nation of no boundaries, yet you live in nations with limitations and systems without freedom. Beware of those things controlling your freedom. Yet you must live by the law you find yourself in, but pray deliverance and diligently tend to the process of freedom in My name, and I will make you free. Verily I say, when you walk in My Nation, you walk free in love. There are no boundaries to My love. No wall can stand up to love. I am a light with no boundaries. Therefore, love is a shade of light.

Not even the tempest can stand up to love, although, she attempts to ensnare those while standing, reaching into their chest and stealing their heart; it is I who prevail, and I give their heart life. Yet, there are those she leaves behind without meaning.

"My day came and went," a young man proclaimed. I walked over to him with light, and said, "How sad is your fate, for you could have been born into eternal life and come as you go, and those of us in such light would know you still, in the eternal life, as someone who comes and goes because they are free. We would know you by your coming, and not so much that you rested, but that you came". I am a light that came and now will return again as God is always. Therefore, My glory is a shade of light.

A gathering of women came out in the day and hid themselves between the rock near a secret pool. The pool was hidden, but the light was not. The water sparkled and shone clear through. None were ashamed of their nakedness while entering the pool. They are closer to never knowing shame, for the holy forever remain in the holy place, and none know shame or guilt. I am a light without shame or quilt. I am the light of confidence and understanding. Therefore, stability is a shade of light. A man whom I came across, was working and laboring to turn his soil, making ready to sow seed. I stopped to ask him of his work, "You are barebacked in this sun, what keeps you from burning?" He replied, "The Son of God." When he went back to work his crops were all planted. He rejoiced. Such joy is a shade of My light.

When the breath of My Spirit comes across the land, some sand will move off the mountain and roll away, and even some of the foundation will move into the sea as a sand hill moves over time. But with the sand that remains, I will build a great mountain. I say to you, be gathered upon the mountain so you are not left behind. See all things spirited in Me upon the land of Israel. A shade of My light is My Spirit. The stone was rolled away from my grave, and I was lifted by His Spirit... All shades of light are in My Father and His Spirit, as I am.

Israel is a shade of My light.

What is constant in My name, Jesus, is My light made whole and complete. So, it is the Morning Star you now see and hear! I am sounding and you can hear. I come to raise My sword against evil. I come to push hate back into the sea. I come to bring about the resurrection of Trinity... to each a task of creation.

I tell you the truth: you have opened the book of these times, now revealed for this time. So it is by My will that it is opened for you to see and hear. The glory is a manifestation, in that it is more full in your ears then before, never more constant than now, never more complete than the beginning, and always the same. None will be left untouched by this, and by touching the remnant, I will come in a cloud of glory over the earth, on a horse of the new light within. The pages of the Book of Life will shine with the book of Daniel and The Rain Bread livened upon My Word at a time the seals begin to open revealing those things of God; in song and in dance, with My Father restored to His domain, I come amongst you, dressed for a wedding and a feast, and His Spirit lifts you, that lifts you to Our high place. I am Jesus, and it is My Word that I give you.

How will I dress myself? I will dress myself with the last remnant and the glory they hold sacred. For there is no finer thread to wear in facing your God.

Appendix

God's Declaration:

I am

I am the Lord Hallow is thy name

I am the Lord your God

I am the one who drops into your midst when you pray in agreement

I am that I am

I am the good shepherd

I am the Son of man

I am the Lord that heals

I am the Son of God

I am the bread of life

I am the light of the world

I am He who searches hearts and minds

I am toward and forward to all who believe in Me

I am the resurrection and the life

I am the first and the last

I am not ashamed of the gospel

I am glad and rejoice with all of you

I am the gate

I am the living bread that came

I am the vine, you are the branches

I am the true vine.

My Scope of Prayer

Author's prayer notes: It is here that I pause and contemplate the things of heaven, which will transpire in the days ahead. I pray this to our Father, Jesus and Holy Spirit, "Hear me oh Lord! I am Praying for no crime and no war among other things such has to each prosperity and health. I no longer doubt it is Jesus Christ that has put forth the light on the word of God for me to guide my own path. And if it can lift another so be it. I pray it give lift and insight where someone benefits. Especially, since Jesus can do this, miracles! I sow these words in faith and pray them in agreement with others as you do in your heart that understands Jesus is alive and He can demonstrate himself in many ways until the day He walks amongst us. I am a voice that prepares His path for His return. Gather He men and hearken unto the Lord, and bring about the gathering and the largest hospitality gathering of its kind. Come, I will show you where He commands you gather. Come to heal the blood of your brother. Come to gather all nations and all tribes. Come to His place and the breath of God will fall upon you and it will refresh. You will see Him in His full dress. He will come and come soon. Amen.

Seven Shades of His Light

Israel

Holy Spirit

Joy

Grace

Glory

Love

Jesus.

www.ingramcontent.com/pod-product-compliance
Lightning Source LLC
Chambersburg PA
CBHW071507040426
42444CB00008B/1538